THE TOY BREEDS

By the same Authors

THE POODLE OWNER'S ENCYCLOPAEDIA

DOGS AND HOW TO SHOW THEM

DOGS AND HOW TO GROOM THEM

VIMS DOG CARE BOOK

POODLES

BREEDING FROM YOUR POODLE

CLIPPING YOUR POODLE

FIRST AID FOR YOUR DOG

FEEDING YOUR POODLE

THE POODLE GUIDE (U.S.A.)

The Toy Breeds

MARGARET SHELDON
&
BARBARA LOCKWOOD

Photographs by Barbara Lockwood

PELHAM BOOKS

7207 0301 8

First published in Great Britain by
PELHAM BOOKS LTD
52 Bedford Square
London W.C.1
1970

7207 0301 8

Printed in Great Britain by
Northumberland Press Limited
Gateshead

CONTENTS

ACKNOWLEDGEMENTS

The Authors wish to acknowledge with grateful thanks the fact that Mr. Charles Binney of the Kennel Club has given permission for the various Standards of the breeds to be reproduced in this book. Also thanks are accorded to the many Toy Dog owners, secretaries of breed clubs and others who have been so generous and helpful with facts and advice.

The authors are aware that most of the dogs mentioned in this book have now gained championship status, but at the time of writing many were still being campaigned for this honour. It was therefore felt that the fairest method was to omit the title 'Ch' in all cases.

ILLUSTRATIONS

1

Toys in General

In these days, the Toy Breeds seem to be increasing in popularity. There are several reasons which may account for this. Firstly, humanity seems to be favouring the smaller house, or flat, with a smaller garden, or sometimes no garden at all. The large dog just would not fit into this way of life but the small toy dog admirably does just that. The price of dog meat has risen beyond all measure, and thus the toy dog eats only a minute percentage of the food normally devoured by the large dog. The toy dog fits comfortably into the modern small car such as the Mini-Minor, and others. Large dogs are frowned on in food shops and on buses, whereas the toy dog can be popped under the arm and hardly noticed. True, the rail fare for a St. Bernard and a tiny Chihuahua is the same, provided neither dog is in a travelling box and thus weighed. Boarding fees have risen in an alarming manner, a large dog costing anything up to 15/- a day, while the toy dog usually gets his accommodation for one-third of this price. So from the economic angle, it would appear that there is good reason for the popularity of the toy dog with the dog-owning public.

But apart from these considerations, many of the Toy Breeds are extremely beautiful. What more lovely than the dignified grandeur of the Pekingese—superciliously royal down to his toe-nails. What more intelligent than the clever, scheming little Toy Poodle. What more incredible than the long shining coat of the Yorkie with his silky hair falling well round his feet and his moustaches (or falls) reaching to the ground. And the snow white Maltese with his top knot often plaited in two Gretchen pigtails and tied with red bows, and the Cavalier and King Charles Spaniels who immediately conjure up pictures of Court life in the 1600's? The Papillons whose ears so resemble the wings of a butterfly. The Toy Breeds are certainly all small dogs in build and weight, but most of them have decided minds of their own and rule their owners with rods of iron. It is not unfair to say that most toy dogs have a tremendous opinion of themselves, and in many cases are extremely vain. They *know* they are superior to all other breeds, and perhaps this applies particularly to the Pekingese. And yet if allowed to be, they are extremely sporting and many equal the terriers in this respect. Above all, they excel in companionship with humans. They *know* how to be friendly, they *know* how to be intensely loyal—and they *know* how to get their own way! Let us not say they are obstinate or even pig headed, but they usually get what they want by sheer tenacity—which all points to great intelligence, doesn't it?

TOY REGISTRATION STATISTICS

It is interesting to study the Toy Registrations over the years. Popularity positions have barely altered during the last five years in the fifteen true toy breeds. (Toy Poodles are not included in these statistics because, although diminutive in size, they do not belong to the Toy Group being officially included in the Non-Sporting Utility Group.) Yorkshire Terriers have, for a great many years, occupied the top place, with Pekingese and Smooth Chihuahuas in second and third places respectively. But in 1968, the Cavalier King Charles Spaniel moved up to 3rd place, pushing the smooth Chihuahua down to 4th place. The only breed to alter position is the Long-Coated Chihuahua which moved up from 8th place in 1964 to 6th place in 1967, pushing the other breeds down a couple of pegs. Cavalier King Charles Spaniels have risen from 1,749 registrations in 1964 to 2,352 in 1967 but this has not affected their position as 4th in the list. In 1968, the number of Italian Greyhounds rose but they were pushed down a place to 14th in spite of this, being superseded by the King Charles Spaniels. More Japanese were registered, and this breed has also climbed two notches to move into 12th place. In the summary given below, total registrations for each breed in each year are given, while the position each year on the list is shown in brackets.

REGISTRATIONS OF TOY BREEDS AT KENNEL CLUB

Breed	*1964*	*1965*	*1966*	*1967*	*1968*
Chihuahua (Smooth Coat)	2691(3)	2701(3)	2595(3)	2436(3)	2502(4)
Chihuahua (Long Coat)	569(8)	720(7)	790(6)	1043(6)	1223(6)
English Toy Terriers	118(15)	118(15)	77(15)	83(15)	72(15)
Griffons Bruxellois	554(9)	459(9)	469(9)	492(9)	547(9)
Italian Greyhounds	140(13)	140(13)	127(14)	119(13)	136(14)
Japanese	121(14)	138(14)	130(13)	116(14)	171(12)
King Charles Spaniels	209(12)	178(12)	159(12)	170(12)	164(13)
Cavalier King Chas. Spans.	1794(4)	1864(4)	2124(4)	2352(4)	2638(3)
Maltese	326(10)	317(10)	327(10)	341(10)	406(10)
Miniature Pinschers	249(11)	244(11)	224(11)	263(11)	226(11)
Papillons	570(7)	585(8)	607(8)	590(8)	753(8)
Pekingese	4421(2)	4205(2)	3502(2)	3774(2)	3980(2)
Pomeranians	722(6)	722(6)	731(7)	767(7)	804(7)
Pugs	1597(5)	1542(5)	1225(5)	1382(5)	1363(5)
Yorkshire Terriers	5531(1)	6129(1)	6306(1)	7389(1)	8842(1)

The following summary shows the position of the four most popular Toys in 'All Breeds Top Twenty'. The remaining eleven Toy Breeds have not yet gained entry to the Top Twenty.

Breed	*1964*	*1965*	*1966*	*1967*	*1968*
Toy Poodles	3rd	3rd	4th	3rd	4th
Yorkshire Terriers	7th	6th	5th	5th	3rd
Pekingese	10th	10th	11th	12th	13th
Smooth Chihuahuas	17th	17th	16th	17th	20th
Cavalier King Charles Spaniels			18th	18th	18th

As will be seen, the Toy Poodle has slipped back to 4th place, giving way to the Yorkshire Terrier who has stepped up to 3rd place in the All Breeds register. The Smooth

Chihuahua is now only just in the Chart in 20th place, and Pekingese have also dropped a place to 13th. The Cavalier King Charles Spaniels have stayed steadily in 18th place. However, some of the Toy Breeds have suffered quite severely from being too popular. This has possibly happened to the Chihuahua, the Yorkie and the Toy Poodle, for all these breeds in their time have been the current 'rage', and the demand has well exceeded the supply. It is a dangerous situation and not one that is in any way to the advantage of the breed, and it brings perturbation to any dog owner who loves his particular breed. An opportunity arises almost overnight to get rich quickly, for puppies are in great demand and prices rise as a result. And so the temptation comes to breed from almost anything irrespective of whether the sire and dam genetically suit each other. Possibly the first generations look all right, but thereafter queer conditions crop-up—blindness in middle age, slipping patellas, hip dysplasia, uncertain tempers, nervousness and the like. Many novices breed puppies of a popular breed because it is obvious there will be no difficulty in selling the puppies and again genetic compatibility is not considered. Very quickly the breed gets a bad name and the only good thing about the situation is that popularity wanes in due course and then the experienced, knowledgeable breeders who have the good of their own breed completely at heart, start to pick up the pieces, and get rid of the bad faults by selective breeding. However, all this takes years and a great deal of harm has been done in the meantime.

Another danger of sudden popularity, especially where the matter of exporting to a foreign country is involved, lies in the well-known 'puppy factories'. Numbers of puppies are bred from sires and dams who are totally unsuited to reproduce themselves. The parents may have a vicious streak or an extremely nervous temperament, but all puppies are sweet at six weeks, and these bad traits will not come out till the puppies are nearly adult, so who cares? Thus, a great many puppies leave the United Kingdom tightly packed in crates. Seldom are such puppies inoculated against disease—vaccines cost money and that would cut down the juicy profits. The usual age for these little globe-trotters is around six to eight weeks although their ages will be given as ten to twelve weeks to comply with the Airline rules. Admittedly they will have been weaned, but their little tummies are unlikely to stand up to a sudden change in diet, and what is more difficult the long interval between meals which must be expected on a lengthy plane flight. Their nerves have been jangled by the rattling and bumping of the transport to the airfield, and the noise of the plane. As a result their tummies are disturbed and they become ill. But these troubles are 'one of those things', and puppies are expendable, it merely means that the profit is not quite so high. And so this mass traffic continues, to the heart-break of all true dog lovers.

Certainly when this situation has developed in any breed the only remedy is the careful selection of breeding pairs, rejection of any dogs or bitches with faulty structure, temperament or stamina, above all well planned breeding programmes which give the bitches plenty of time for rest and recuperation between litters.

CHOOSING THE RIGHT PUPPY

So now we come to the question of what to look for when buying a toy puppy. Obviously the standard of the particular breed should be read and re-read so that the desired points can be recognised, and also faults quickly noticed. Each breed has its own special attributes, and it is only proposed to point out in this chapter the superficial points to be sure about when buying a new puppy. Firstly, cleanliness. Check that the puppy you are viewing is clean—looks clean, feels clean and smells clean. Look well at the eyes for they should be clear and bright. Beware of the puppy with deep, limpid, dull eyes for this means that he is not a one hundred per cent fit, that he may have worms, or that he has been shut up in a small dark kennel with little chance to develop his natural intelligence. Check his back parts, and if there is any redness or soreness, be careful for this usually means diarrhoea or some unhealthiness. As to temperament, the puppy who comes to you of his own accord, nibbles your fingers, unties your shoe laces, and generally romps around you has no temperament problems. But the puppy who hangs back and sidles into a corner, or is frightened when picked up, is not very promising. He may be sweet now, and you may be sorry for him as he is quiet and gentle, but this nervousness will increase as he gets older. If possible ask to see the sire and dam. Much can be learned from the temperament of the parent stock. If you wish to do so, ask your Veterinary Surgeon to check the puppy before you buy—but you, as the buyer, must pay for this and usually the seller or breeder of the puppy would not let the puppy go unless fully insured, and the insurance premium would be your responsibility.

Many toy breeds have been bred down to a diminutive size from a larger size, for often the smaller the puppy the more valuable it is. But don't forget that the very small puppies often carry faults caused by the dwarfing process. For instance, an undershot jaw happens because the top jaw has reduced more than the lower jaw; front legs are sometimes a fraction shorter than hind legs; large prominent eyes in those breeds which call for a flat, small eye may occur because eyes are the most difficult features to breed down in size. Fragility of bones often goes hand in hand with the tiniest toys, so a little heavier bone may be an advantage. Also the tiniest bitches of any toy breed may not be large enough to breed successfully, without Caesarian section, so possibly a slighter larger specimen would be an advantage. On the other hand, a tiny male dog will manage his duties as a stud force perfectly adequately, and so a tiny puppy destined as a future stud dog is an advantage. There is no guarantee as to what size a six- or eight-week-old puppy will attain at maturity except that most toy puppies follow the size of their parents, but quite a good guide is in the size of nose and also size of feet. Big nostrils and big feet usually mean a bigger puppy.

SHOW PREPARATION

There are, of course, many small ways in which a dog's looks can be enhanced in the show ring, but tips about such matters are usually only picked up from the 'old hands' who have been 'in' the relevant breed for many, many years. Certainly when the novice takes up a breed, he or she will need to know how to prepare the chosen breed to the best advantage and many of the particularly beautifully coated toy breeds such as the Pekingese, the Maltese and the Yorkie need tremendous knowledge, energy and 'know-how'. None of these fabulously-coated breeds are easy and usually weeks of most careful grooming and trimming are necessary before the show date. It really isn't possible to walk into the ring and expect to win with such breeds without any previous knowledge of how to prepare the coat. The technique is far too involved. One must serve one's apprenticeship, and during such time it pays handsomely to watch the experts preparing their dogs, and to keep one's ears and eyes open to take in new methods and worthwhile techniques. Most experienced show people are extremely kind to novice exhibitors when help and advice is asked, but the right moment of approach must be sought. Don't expect any attention when an exhibitor is just on the point of taking his or her dog into the ring. He would be a saint if he could attend at that moment. Dog-showing to most exhibitors is a very serious business and quite a lot of stress is involved. In fact, with some it is almost a matter of life and death. The best time to ask advice is when the exhibitor has completed his classes for the day, has possibly won well, has refreshed both himself and his dog, and is feeling pleased with the world in general. That is the psychological moment when the expert will generally give all possible help to the novice.

There are of course, many toy breeds which need rather less show preparation. The short-coated Chihuahua, the Miniature Pinscher, the Pug, the Italian Greyhound are all comparatively simple to prepare. But of course you may hanker for the long exotic coat which provides a tremendous challenge—and a heck of a lot of grinding hard work! However, providing you are prepared to work on your show dogs for every hour of the day and every day of the week you will certainly succeed. Show preparation is certainly not a pastime through which one can drift lazily. Few spectators know the tremendous effort that has been put into a dog to bring him to the top of the Best-in-Show ring. But how well worthwhile it is, and when it happens, all the trials and tribulations melt away. Immense satisfaction and tremendous pride in your beloved dog is then paramount. And the day after the show you will still finger those Challenge Certificates, Rosettes and Silver Cups and walk on air—and are dead beat!

Rules which apply to the preparation of all breeds are these: (1) Groom your dog daily. (2) Use only the best shampoos, conditioners, tools and equipment. (3) Feed your show dogs on the best quality food to achieve that desired bloom and shine of coat. (4) Exercise judicially to keep the muscles taut and the skin flexible. (5) Train constantly in ring craft. (6) Make grooming and training periods times of pleasure and not of boredom or discomfort.

Make the show day a time of pleasurable anticipation, real enjoyment and comfort. Your dog is helping you to enjoy yourself so he is entitled to his share of the pleasure. Showing *can* be pleasant for him if you put yourself out to make it so. The whole affair then becomes a partnership and it is surprising what great companionship thus can be achieved between man and dog. So often an exhibitor appears to take the full credit for the show successes that come his way—and yet what could he do without his dog!

Above: CHIHUAHUA (Long coated). Showing the long coat and the feathering at the back of the front legs, back of thighs and tail. Also the rounded apple dome of the skull between the widely spaced ears. *Below:* CHIHUAHUA (Short coated). This variety has a close and glossy coat, and the typical moderately short and slightly pointed nose.

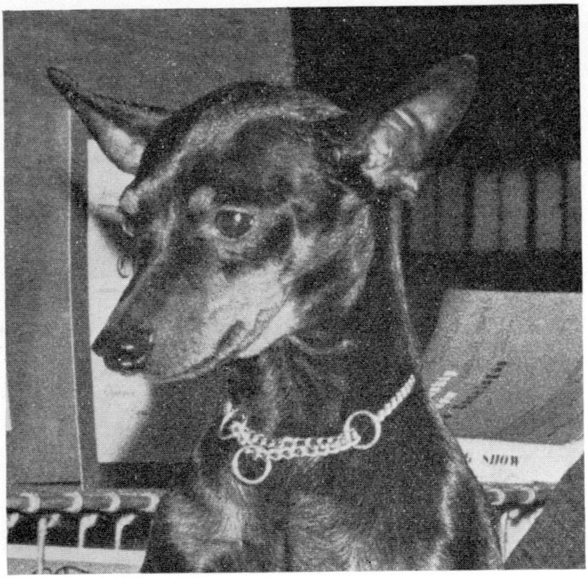

Above: ENGLISH TOY TERRIER (Black and Tan). Lancer of Leospride, owned by Mrs. Boud. This picture shows the long, narrow, wedge-shaped head with tight-lipped jaws, and a moderately long neck tapering from the shoulders to the head. *Below:* ENGLISH TOY TERRIER (Black and Tan). He has a close, smooth and glossy coat with well defined black and tan markings. The black must not run into the tan, nor *vice versa*, and the division between the two colours must be clear cut.

2

Chihuahuas

As his name suggests, this alert, spry litle dog stems from Chihuahua in Mexico. Many people are quite convinced that the Chihuahua was a definite breed of dog primarily evolved by the priests of the Aztec Empire more than 1,000 years ago, and used by them for religious sacrifices. Other writers discount this theory completely and cling fondly to the opinion that the Chihuahua was first brought to Mexico by the Chinese, and therefore is a Chinese dog, while others have proved to themselves, if not to the many Chihuahua breeders, that they are really crossed Papillons! It has even been suggested that this little dog was at some time used as a tasty culinary addition! There is still another theory that Chihuahuas are descended from the Fennec Fox, which was a native of the Sahara Desert, carnivorous and also a nocturnal animal. Therefore it seems almost impossible to come to any definite conclusion as to their true origin. Suffice it to say that they certainly do not enter into the history of English dogs, only the odd one being seen in this country before the early 1920's.

A Breed Club was founded in 1949, but it was not until 1954 that Chihuahuas were officially recognised as a separate breed by the Kennel Club. Even after this, Chihuahuas were rarely seen until about 1963 when they suddenly became the rage and quickly mounted to third place in the Toy registrations, being surpassed only by Yorkies and Pekingese. There are now two varieties in England, the smooth-coated and the long-coated and these were separately scheduled for the first time at Crufts in 1965. The two varieties have been recognised for far longer in the United States of America, and in Western Australia the two different coats now have been split into two separate varieties—indeed, in that country a long-coated puppy born to smooth-coated parents may not even be registered.

There is no doubt at all that the Chihuahua is a charming little animal, alert, intelligent, with a great and loving heart. He adores to be nursed and cuddled, possibly because he is a dog who suffers greatly from the cold. This applies particularly to the smooth-coated variety, for he has practically nothing extra to keep him warm. In spite of this, he is a little dog who is always full of himself, completely independent and indeed extremely robust.

The official Standard of the Breed as laid down by the Kennel Club is as follows:

CHIHUAHUA (SMOOTH COAT)

CHARACTERISTICS—An alert and swift-moving little dog with a saucy expression.

GENERAL APPEARANCE—Small, dainty and compact with a brisk, forceful action.

Head and Skull—A well-rounded 'Apple Dome' skull with or without Molero, cheeks and jaws lean, nose moderately short, slightly pointed. Definite stop.

Eyes—Full, round but not protruding, set well apart, dark or ruby. (Light eyes in light colours permissible.)

Ears—Large, set on at an angle of about 45 degrees; this gives breadth between the ears.

Mouth—Level, scissor bite.

Neck—Slightly arched, of medium length.

Forequarters—Shoulders should be well up, lean, sloping into a slightly broadening support above straight forelegs that are set well under, giving free play at the elbows.

Body—Level back, slightly longer than the height at the shoulder. Well sprung ribs with deep brisket.

Hindquarters—Muscular with hocks well apart, neither out nor in, well let down.

Feet—Small with toes well split up, but not spread, pads cushioned. Fine pasterns (neither 'Hare' nor 'Cat' foot). A dainty foot with nails moderately long.

Tail—Medium length carried up or over the back. Preferred furry, flattish in appearance, broadening slightly in the centre and tapering to a point.

Coat—Smooth, of soft texture, close and glossy.

Colour—Any colour or mixture of colours.

Weight—Up to six pounds, with two to four pounds preferable. If two dogs are equally good in type, the more diminutive preferred.

Faults—Cropped tail, brokendown ears.

CHIHUAHUA (LONG COAT)

The Standard of the Chihuahua (Long Coat) is the same as the Standard of the Chihuahua (Smooth Coat) with the exception of the following:

Coat—Long, of soft texture (never coarse or harsh to the touch) either flat or slightly wavy. No tight curly coat. There should be feathering on the feet and legs, pants on the hind legs, a large ruff on the neck is desired and preferred, the tail should be long and full as a plume.

The Chihuahua is a tiny dog, often said to be the smallest in the world, weighing around 2 to 4 lbs.; and certainly not over 6 lbs. Any colour or mixture of colours is permissible.

The grooming of the smooth-coated Chihuahua is by no means onerous. Brushing daily with a fairly soft short-haired brush will keep the coat clean and in good healthy condition, and the grooming session should be completed by steady polishing with a piece of velvet or silk or a soft corduroy 'glove'. Bathing is seldom necessary but the coats will benefit considerably if given the 'Charbon' Treatment. 'Charbon' is an excellent shampoo prepared by Vitacoat Ltd., of Selsdon

Road, Croydon. Half a teaspoon of 'Charbon' Shampoo is added to a quart of warm water. A sponge is then soaked in this liquid and *half* wrung-out. The coat is then wiped down, and the sponge rinsed-out as necessary. Once again, the sponge is soaked in the liquid and wrung-out *almost* dry, and again the coat is wiped. Any further rinsing is unnecessary, and the procedure is completed with a brisk rub down with a dry cloth or a chamois leather. This obviates an actual bath and drying time is very much reduced which is a great advantage with little dogs who feel the cold and are really short coated.

The long-coated Chihuahua needs a little extra brushing and combing of the longer fringed areas of the coat, and a bath when necessary. General purpose shampoos such as Vitacoat 'Anti-scurf' or 'Olivite' are both perfectly suitable for the longer coated variety.

The smooth-coated variety needs little or no special trimming but as he is meant to *be* smooth, the whiskers on the muzzle and the eyebrows should be kept cleanly snipped-off with scissors, while any longer hairs at the side of the neck or the underside of the tail should also be kept tidily short. The fringing on the long-coated varieties on legs, side of neck and tail should be scissored-off slightly to make an even finish. The above remarks apply to the routine maintenance required to keep the pet or companion Chihuahua in smart condition. The preparation needed for the top show dog entails specialised knowledge by the expert in the breed and in any case there is not enough space in a book of this size to describe the show preparation techniques of all the lovely Toy breeds.

This chapter about Chihuahuas would not be complete without some details of recent show winners. The British Chihuahua Club usually holds its Championship Show in February or March of each year, and the Challenge Certificate winning dogs and bitches are noted over the last five years, together with the name of the officiating judge. The same details are given for Chihuahuas at Crufts for the last six years.

The British Chihuahua Club was founded in 1949, and amongst those responsible for this Club were Mrs. Joan C. Forster, Mrs. M. Fearfield and Mrs. Dora Wells. Members now number over 600 and the secretary is Mr. L. F. S. Baker of 64 Westbourne Gardens, Hove, Sussex. There is a most interesting Club magazine published quarterly which is called *Chihuahua Chatter* and this is free to members.

At the general Championship Shows up and down the country both smooth- and long-coated Chihuahuas have featured among the winning dogs of all breeds, notably, Strondour Valdama Sweet Memory who was piloted by her owner Mrs. Walker, after winning Best of Breed, to a place in the finals of the Toy Group at Crufts. Montesuma Mr. Chips, owned by Mrs. Horton-Hall also did very well by being judged Best Dog in Show at the Long Coat Club Show, while Lady Drummond-Hay's Seggieden Tiny Mite has been awarded well over twenty Challenge Certificates. At the Three Counties Championship Show, Mrs. Gagen's Lilycroft Penny Lane gained Reserve Best Toy, while Mrs. Ryder's Rowley Uvalda Winston gained the same honour at Dumfries Championship Show. Many other Chihuahuas have taken the top places, notably Rowley Copyrite, Rowley Josephine, Jofos Kitty's Little Joe, Larkwhistle Vanilla, Rozavel Cadbury, Wingreen Aphrodite, Venico Memento, Rozavel Astra, Dekobras Danny Boy, Chitina's Nixtrix Prince Charming (Long-Coat) and Maidenslea Nephthys (Smooth-Coat), these last two being Best of Breed respectively at Crufts, 1969.

Unfortunately Chihuahuas suffered a little from their rapid popularity in the mid-60's which resulted in the breeding of a great number with perhaps not always due regard to the suitability and soundness of the parent stock. However, the really conscientious breeder is quickly bringing soundness back to the breed and the little 'Chi' is slowly and surely

THE BRITISH CHIHUAHUA CLUB CHAMPIONSHIP SHOW

Year	*Dog Challenge Certificate*	*Bitch Challenge Certificate*	*Judge*
1964	Seggieden Mighty Dime	Snowdrop of Glenjoy	Mr. F. Cross
1965	Jofos Jim Dandy	Rediviva Garicia (S/C)	Mrs. M. Fearfield
1966	Rozavel Alfonso Zapangu (L/C)	Deodar Honey Dew (L/C)	Mrs. E. Basset
	Lilycroft Son of Fortune (S/C)	Rowley Ruby of Daleavon (S/C)	
1967	Winterlea Lone Wolf (L/C)	Rowley Kismet (L/C)	Miss D. R. Allen
	Rozavel Chief Scout (S/C)	Winterlea Twinkle of Mingulay	Mrs. M. Huxham
1968	Dekobras Danny Boy (L/C)	Rozavel Astra (L/C)	Miss S. Jones
	Jofos Kitty's Little Joe (S/C)	Rowley Lansdahlia Candytuft (S/C)	Mr. L. Baker

CRUFTS CHAMPIONSHIP SHOW (CHIHUAHUAS)

1964	Emmrill Fudge	Snowdrop of Glenjoy	Mrs. T. Gray
1965	Seggieden Mighty Dime	Tinkerbell of Glenjoy (S/C)	Mrs. J. Rawson
1966	Winterlea Lone Wolf (L/C)	Lansdahlia Talaloc Twinkle (L/C)	Mrs. Foster
	Rosavel Chief Scout (S/C)	Rowley Josephine (S/C)	
1967	Pequeno Little Caesar (L/C)	Rowley Kismet (L/C)	Mr. S. Young
	Dalhabboch Alfy (S/C)	Candifloss of Wychend (S/C)	Mrs. M. Mooney
1968	Venico Memento (L/C)	Wingreen Aphrodite (L/C)	Mrs. T. Gray
	Salsam Don Carlos (S/C)	Strondour Valdama Sweet Memory	Mrs. J. Foster
1969	Chitina's Nixtrix Prince Charming (L/C)	Rozavel Tarina Song (L/C)	Mrs. M. Huxham
	Salsom Don Carlos (S/C)	Maidenslea Nephthys (S/C)	Mrs. Ellis-Hughes

The Scottish and Northern Counties Chihuahua Club also hold a Championship Show about October in each year.

becoming the healthy, robust, well-made little dog who justly merits his popularity. Mr. Baker, the Secretary of the Chihuahua Club summed-up the breed neatly by saying, 'He is a sprightly, gay little dog, full of life, brave as a lion and very affectionate. He is mainly a one-man or one-woman dog.'

3

English Toy Terrier (Black and Tan)

This is a breed which is essentially English as its name implies, for there is nothing of any other country in its forebears. He sprang from the old-time hunting terriers and is a keen ratter, in fact, he was used in the rat pits in the north of England in the 1800's when rat killing, cock fighting and the like were occasions for lively gambling. He was formerly known as the Black-and-Tan Terrier, but is now re-named the English Toy Terrier.

A sharp, strong, intelligent little terrier weighing under 8 lbs. Still a splendid ratter and mouser, an excellent guard dog for his size, and always on the tips of his toes and ready for anything, but preferably hunting.

The colour of the English Toy Terrier is particularly attractive. The black must be shiny coal black while the tan must be a really deep colour, and neither must run into the other. The dividing lines must be very pronounced.

In the olden days some of these Black-and-Tans produced all tan puppies, or indeed whole litters which were bright tan coloured, and these puppies were tremendously sought after. Even now, completely tan litters may turn up very, very rarely. Also occasionally puppies appear with white patches, though usually such patches disappear quite quickly. They are said to be throw-backs to the English Fox Terrier, and the patch is usually on the chest. Needless to say, puppies with white patches could not be presented in the show-ring and should only be sold as pets.

The official Standard of the breed as laid down by the

Kennel Club gives much attention to coat colour. Here it is:

ENGLISH TOY TERRIER (BLACK AND TAN)

GENERAL APPEARANCE—A well balanced, elegant and compact Toy with Terrier temperament and characteristics. It must be borne in mind that in the past the breed was required frequently to be able to acquit itself satisfactorily in the rat pit. Therefore present day specimens should be sleek and cleanly built giving an appearance of alertness combined with speed of movement but not of whippet type.

In realisation of the fact that this is a Toy Dog with Terrier characteristics, unduly nervous specimens cannot rank as wholly typical representatives of the breed. Judges, when officiating, should bear this in mind.

Head and Skull—The head should be long and narrow with a flat skull, wedge-shaped without emphasis of cheek muscles and well filled-up under the eyes. The top and bottom jaws should be held tightly together within compressed lips. Upon close inspection of the foreface one finds indication of a slight 'stop'. The foreface then tapers gently to provide a wedge-shaped impression in profile similarly corresponding to that given when it is viewed direct. Although an illusion of being 'overshot' can result, any suggestion of a snipey appearance is undesirable. *Nose*—Black.

Eyes—These should be very dark to black without light shading from the iris. They should be small, almond shaped, obliquely set and sparkling.

N.B.—Light, large and round, protruding or disproportionately wide or narrow set eyes should be regarded as faults.

Ears—These should be of 'candle-flame' shape, slightly pointed at the tips, placed high upon the back of the skull and proportionately close together. A guide to the size can be obtained by bending the ear forward. It should not reach the eye. From nine months of age the ear carriage must be erect. The entire inside of the ear should face the front. The leather of the ear should be thin. A cat ear appearance is wrong.

N.B.—Large or 'flapping' ears should be regarded as faults.

Mouth—Teeth should be level and strong. The upper front teeth should close slightly over the lower front teeth, the latter to lean forward fractionally thus establishing the correct level bite.

Neck—The neck should be long, graceful, and slightly arched. The shoulders should be well laid back not straight. The pattern of the neck line flowing into the shoulders, and sloping off elegantly. Throatiness is undesirable.

Forequarters—The chest narrow and deep. Legs falling straight from the shoulders, with the elbows close to the chest providing a straight front. Loose elbows and wide fronts are faults. Fine bone is eminently desirable. The ideal fore-movement is that akin to the 'extended trot', hackney action is not desirable; equally to be discouraged is a 'shuffling' gait.

Body—The body is compact, head and legs proportionate thus producing correct balance. The back very slightly curving from behind the shoulder to the loin falling again to the root of the tail. The chest should be narrow and deep with the ribs well sprung to a well cut-up loin. The buttocks should be gently rounded.

Faults—A roached, dipped or dead flat back, hindquarters higher than the shoulders.

Hindquarters—A well-rounded loin leading to a good turn of stifle is required, hocks well let down, a 'tucked under' appearance is undesirable. Hind-action should be smooth and suggest ease and precision combined with drive. There should be a 'flowing quality' to give true soundness.

Feet—Dainty compact, split-up between the toes, and well arched, with jet black nails; the two middle toes of the front feet rather longer than the others and the hind feet shaped like those of a cat. Hare feet are not desirable, and should be regarded as a fault.

Tail—The tail should be thick at the root, tapering to a point. Set low and not reaching below the hock. A 'gay' tail carriage is undesirable if displayed to excess.

Coat—The texture should be thick, close, smooth and of glossy appearance. A density of short hair is required. *N.B.*—Sparse, weak coats should be regarded as faults.

Colour—Black and Tan. The black should be ebony and the tan can be likened to a new chestnut, deeply rich. These colours should not run, or blend into each other, but should meet abruptly, forming clear and well defined lines of colour division. Forelegs tanned to the knee in front. The tan then continuing inside and at the back of the foreleg to a point just below the elbow. A thin black line up each toe (Pencilling) and a clearly defined black mark 'thumb mark' on the centre of each pastern, and under the chin. The hind legs should be well tanned in front and the inside, with a black 'bar' dividing the tan at the centre of the lower thigh. Each toe 'pencilled'. Heavy tan on the outside of the hindquarters, 'breeching', is a fault. On the head the muzzle is well tanned, nose black, the black continuing along the top of the muzzle, curving below the eyes to the base of the throat. A tan spot above each eye and a small tan spot on each cheek. The under jaw and throat are tanned, the lip line black. The hair inside the ears tanned (tan behind the ears a fault). Each side of the chest is slightly tanned. The vent and under root of the tail tanned. White hairs forming a patch anywhere are a serious fault.

Weight and Size—The ideal weight is between that of 6-8 lbs. and a height of 10-12 inches at the shoulders is most desirable.

Judges are encouraged to use scales, as it is hoped this will help to establish uniformity.

Most people having read the Standard, will agree that the uniformity of marking is most interesting. A really well marked English Toy Terrier is a beautiful picture. The small black thumb mark above the toes with the thin black pencil lines running-up each tan toe, the small tan 'V' under the tail, and the bright spot on each cheek and just above each eye. Seldom is any other breed so symmetrically adorned! The ears of this terrier were originally cropped but it is many years since this practice was stopped by law on humane grounds. The ear carriage must now be erect after the age of nine months.

Coats are easy to groom. Health is the paramount factor, for if the dog is well fed, warmly and cleanly housed, and completely free of all parasites such as fleas, lice and worms, his coat will have that much sought-after bloom. Regular grooming with a fibre glove, followed by polishing with either velvet, corduroy or a silk handkerchief or cloth will produce the result that is needed. While the sheen and gloss can be achieved by these means, the correct placement of the marking and also the clarity and depth of the colour is usually a matter of breeding—and very selective breeding at that. It will have been handed down through the generations, so look to the parents, grandparents and so on for these assets when buying a puppy.

The English Toy Terrier (Black and Tan) Club is a flourishing affair and holds a yearly Championship Club Show generally in September. The Challenge Certificate Winners for the past five years at this show are given on the opposite page.

It would seem that Mrs. Green's Rajah of Ivycourt held a very impregnable position, and was obviously the considered choice of Specialist and All-Round judges alike. More recently Mrs. Elliott's lovely little bitch Anin Solo Advent has carried-off the Best in Show award at the Club Championship Show in both 1967 and 1968, and was also judged English Toy Terrier of the year in 1967, having gained her Junior Warrant early that year. Mrs. Bond's Lancer of Leospride is another outstanding English Toy Terrier who seems to improve every time he is shown. Mrs. Voce with her dainty, vivacious little bitch Bordesley Bowbells has hit the

THE ENGLISH TOY TERRIER (BLACK AND TAN) CLUB CHAMPIONSHIP SHOW

Year	*Dog Challenge Certificate*	*Bitch Challenge Certificate*	*Judge*
1964	Rajah of Ivycourt	Quaker Girl	Miss L. G-Weall
1965	Rajah of Ivycourt	Bordesley Bow Bells	Mr. S. McKie
1966	Rajah of Ivycourt	Bordesley Bow Bells	Mr. Speight
1967	Flute of Lenster	Anin Solo Advent	Mr. G. Couzens
1968	Lancer of Leospride	Anin Solo Advent	Mr. J. Scholes

And here are the winners at Crufts Show over the years:

CRUFTS CHAMPIONSHIP SHOW (ENGLISH TOY TERRIERS)

1964	Rajah of Ivycourt	Quaker Girl	Miss L. G-Weall
1965	Rajah of Ivycourt	Joyjeans Juno	Mr. L. Radford
1966	Rajah of Ivycourt	Quaker Girl	Mr. Fullwood
1967	Bordesley Sunny Jim	Bordesley Bow Bells	Mrs. Warner-Hill
1968	Rajah of Ivycourt	Bordesley Bow Bells	Miss L. G-Weall
1969	Lancer of Leospride	Stealaway Golden Girl	Mr. E. Speight

headlines and has a string of Challenge Certificates to her credit.

The English Toy Terrier also has the distinction of being an actual resident of the Kennel Club, for Mrs. Bond, who is the wife of the House Manager of the Kennel Club in Piccadilly owns Danny Boy of Cherrycroft, a very well bred and attractive member of the English Toy Terrier breed.

Those exhibitors who are also well up in the awards at a great many of the Championship Shows are Miss Bentley (Benhelmstone), Mrs. Edwards (Scarteen), Mrs. Hunt with her Quaker Girl; and Mrs. Mankin and Miss Scovell (Lenster).

Unfortunately, the English Toy Terrier occupies last place in the fifteen members of the Toy Group, and even more sadly registrations are dropping every year, now descending to a mere 83, while in both 1959 and 1961 the figures were a healthy 184. And yet could one find a more sporting, brave, lovable little dog than this sporting terrier? We are told to 'Back Britain'—should this not include the delightful English Toy Terrier?

4

Griffons Bruxellois

Everyone who has owned a Griffon is quite convinced that this breed outshines any other type of dog. There seems to be a mystical quality in the Griffon which insists on slavery from a mere human. These little dogs are angels and devils rolled into one, and yet at times can be completely disdainful and supercilious, and at others the most generous in their wealth of devotion and affection. But one thing they will never do—and that is fawn. They go their own way with the sweetest possible manners!

As with so many of the Toy Breeds, the origin of the Griffon is wrapped in mystery and doubt. The word 'Griffon' means rough-coated, and so could apply to many breeds. The date of 1880 seems to be the first time Griffons were noted as such, though rough-coated little dogs which have something (though very little) in common with the Griffon as we know him, have been written about since the fifteenth century. There is a painting in the National Gallery by Van Eck dated 1434 called *The Marriage of Giovanni Arnolfini and Giovanna Cenami* in which a small dog appears which is purported by many to be a Griffon. However, this little dog has the characteristics more of a cairn, or at any rate a sporting terrier with a long and slightly wavy coat, and with a nose considerably longer than the snub-nose we connect with the Griffon. As many canine historians have advanced theories that the Griffon stemmed from the Affen Pinscher and the Yorkshire Terrier, this might explain the nose resemblance. Griffons are also said to have been evolved by crossing such breeds as Pugs and Toy Spaniels. They certainly are a breed with little class consciousness, for in their early days they were great favourites of the Queen of the Belgians in the late 19th century, having before that been the constant companions of the Brussels hackney coachmen who used them extensively for ratting.

It does appear that true to their name they originally came from Belgium. There are two types, namely Griffon Bruxellois (the rough coated) and Petit Brabançon (the smooth).

The original official Standard of the breed was amended in 1959, and as will be seen includes quite a formidable list of faults which prevent a dog from winning a prize. Some of these faults have been handed down over the generations—for example, the forbidden silky hair on top of the head which is said may have come from the introduction of the Yorkshire Terrier. Although not mentioned in the Standard, webbed feet are, or were, a great bug-bear. They have now been for the most part bred-out of the present day Griffon, but still the odd web-foot does occur, and this is said to be a legacy from the Belgian Toy Spaniels.

Here is the Standard of the breed as laid down by the Kennel Club:

GRIFFONS BRUXELLOIS

CHARACTERISTICS—There are two types—the Griffon Bruxellois which is rough and the Petit Brabançon which is smooth. The Griffon is a small dog with a Terrier-like temperament.

GENERAL APPEARANCE—Well balanced, cobby body, intelligent expression, lively and alert.

Head and Skull—Head should be large and rounded but in no way domed, and should be wide between the ears. Hair on the skull, in the rough variety, should be rather coarse. Nose always black, as short as possible, with large open nostrils, high set, and sloping back to the skull with a deep stop between nose and skull. Wide muzzle with good turn up; chin prominent and slightly undershot without showing

Above: GRIFFON BRUXELLOIS. Polrose Personality Plus, owned by Mrs. Gregory. A large round head, wide between the ears, with rather expressive dark eyes, and a profuse, coarse beard. *Below:* ITALIAN GREYHOUND. Oxslip Felicity, owned by Mrs. Day. A small toy breed, weight around eight pounds, with a bright and expressive eye, a long flat skull and fine muzzle.

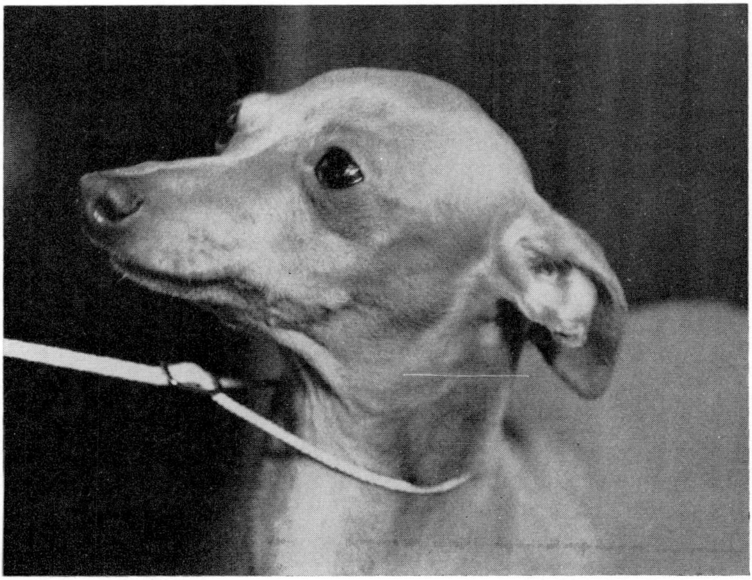

Above: JAPANESE. Weycombe Verbena and Michiko of Yevot, owned by Miss Tovey. Two outstandingly lovely Japanese showing the broad head, and the short muzzle which is well cushioned. The much desired show of white at the inner corner of the eye, giving a somewhat astonished look, is very evident here. *Below:* JAPANESE. Three delightful Japanese peeping out from their show pen at Crufts Championship Show. They are owned by Mrs. Tovey.

teeth, and (in the rough variety) furnished with a beard.

Eyes—Large, round, black or nearly black, with black eye-rims.

Ears—Semi-erect, high set, the smaller the better.

Mouth—Slightly undershot and teeth regular.

Neck—Of medium length and slightly arched.

Forequarters—Chest rather wide and deep; legs straight, of medium length with good bone.

Body—Short back, well sprung ribs and shoulder well laid back. The back should be level from the point of shoulder to tail; it should not be roached, nor should it dip to the shoulder.

Hindquarters—Strong and muscular, thighs of medium length, hocks well bent.

Feet—Small cat-like feet with black toe nails.

Tail—Roughly two-thirds docked, set on high.

Coat—Roughs—harsh and wiry, free from curl. Smooths—short and smooth.

Colour—Clear red, black, or black and rich tan.

Weight and Size—From 3 lbs. to 10 lbs. Most desirable, 6 to 9 lbs.

Faults—Silky hair on top of head; showing teeth or tongue; overshot or wry mouth; light eyes; brown nose, eye-rims or toe-nails; curly coat. The following faults should prevent a dog from winning a prize: brown nose; white patches; wry mouth; tongue protruding. Coats cut with scissors should also be penalised.

The grooming and show preparation of the rough-coated Griffon is difficult and needs much skill, while that of the Petit Brabançon (smooth-coated) is comparatively easy. To take the rough-coated variety first, these will need daily brushing with a stiffish bristle brush, and combing with a chromium-plated brass comb, fairly fine toothed. The coat should be stripped-out with the finger and thumb method twice a year, when the top coat is dead and falling. The stripping of the show dog is more complicated as the removal of hair must be carried-out at the very right moment. Since the hair should be longer on top of neck, back, hindquarters and back of forelegs it must be stripped first. But on the sides of the neck, shoulders, brisket and sides of body and thighs the hair is required to be shorter, so it will need stripping nearer to the show period. As it is necessary for the top harsh coat to cover the soft undercoat, it is realised why both the use of scissors or electric clippers are not permissible. Both the latter will not take out the roots of the dead hair but will simply cut through. The coat must start with a well stripped undercoat, and the Griffon will be in perfect coat fettle when this undercoat his grown-up harshly to the required length. The coat must above all be rough and harsh, but never shaggy.

The beard is left really long with whiskers sticking out stiffly. Don't comb too often—only often enough to keep smart and sanitary. The ears must be very closely stripped by finger and thumb, but the head must never be over-trimmed as it should give the impression of being massive. This description of the trimming of the Griffon only skirts the subject, and obviously it takes years of experience to put down this breed to perfection. As the coat must be harsh, bathing is not undertaken too often, for that will only soften the coat. The 'Charbon' Treatment as described for Chihuahuas is excellent for both the rough and the smooth types. For the latter, a rather softer brush is used, and the coat is polished with a silk handkerchief or velvet glove until it gleams.

The Griffon Bruxellois breeders formed their own breed club in 1893. The name of the actual founder seems to be obscure but Miss Gordon is named as the first Honorary Secretary. It was not until some twenty years later that the Club held its first breed show. Sir Howard and Lady Spicer, Miss Gordon and Mrs. Kinscote all worked extremely hard in the early days to get the breed successfully on its way. Only 3 Griffons were registered in 1898 but in 1961 registrations reached a total of 616. Over the last few years, registrations have been slightly down, decreasing to a total of 492 in 1967. They have, however, consistently maintained their position of 9th in the Toy Breeds Popularity Poll over the last five years.

The Griffon Club is flourishing and has a membership of some 250 enthusiastic Griffon breeders. An excellent handbook is published which is distributed free to members, and is available to non-members at a charge of 10/6d. A Championship Club Show is usually held around April each year, and the Challenge Certificate winners at this show over the last five years are shown overleaf.

Among Griffons dogs which have distinguished themselves lately, in addition to the successes overleaf, are Mrs. Dixon's red rough Oscar of Otterbourne, and the Misses Gregory's black rough Black Arrow of Gregtoi; and among the bitches, Mr. Barker's red rough Antees Amoretta, Mrs. H. Wolstenholme's black rough Glenalda Gi-Gi, and Mr. Gregory's rough black-and-tan Chosendale Pennicandy of Tunlake. Mrs. Street of the Skibbereen Griffons, has been particularly successful for she has made up no less than twenty-four champions and is holder of over 170 Challenge Certificates—an achievement entailing a great deal of hard work and devotion to the breed, and she always seems to produce the best Griffon at Crufts, for this honour has come her way for the last five years.

A word about the colour of Griffons. The Standard lays down that this should be clear red, black, or black and rich tan. Such colours as blue, chocolate (or liver colour), brindle or fawn are not desirable at all. The rough reds are by far the most popular and the most numerous, with the smooth reds next, closely followed by the rough blacks. The smooth blacks are not very popular as pets, though favoured by breeders quite considerably. Black-and-tans, though most attractive, are seldom seen these days. As a general rule, the rough seems to be more frequently amongst the winners, and

THE GRIFFONS BRUXELLOIS CLUB CHAMPIONSHIP SHOW

Year	*Dog Challenge Certificate*	*Bitch Challenge Certificate*	*Judge*
1964	Ruskington Remy	Brabjoy Samantha	Mrs. J. Cottrell
1965	Brutus of Margidunum	Skibbereen Alexandra	Mrs. E. Basset
1966	Gay Cavalier of Kirkmarland	Glenalda Gi-gi	Miss A. Tyler
1967	Black Arrow of Gregtoi	Chosendale Pennicandy of Tunlake	Mr. P. Whitaker
1968	Baratelle Red Robin	Star Charmer of Gregtoi	Mrs. Fearfield

And here are the winners at Crufts over the years:

CRUFTS CHAMPIONSHIP SHOW (GRIFFONS BRUXELLOIS)

1964	Thatchway Cruiser	Gaystock La Fable	Mrs. Fearfield
1965	Playboy Simon	Skibbereen Alexandra	Mrs. W. Barber
1966	Gay Cavalier of Kirkmarland	Skibbereen Alexandra	Mr. Dangerfield
1967	Gyantze Goldenglory	Skibbereen Brabjoy Estralita	Mr. Warner-Hill
1968	Keitoy Kismet	Skibbereen Brabjoy Estralita	Mrs. Barter
1969	Keitoy Kismet	Skibbereen Panache Mona Lisa	Mrs. J. Cottrell

it appears very much more difficult to catch the judge's eye with a smooth. It is possible to have both rough and smooth puppies in one litter, for many breeders mate rough and smooth types together as this is believed to benefit the coat texture in resulting puppies. A proportion of smooth puppies may even occur in an all-rough mating, though if two smooths are mated together it is unlikely that this will produce any roughs. Reds and blacks are less often mated together, for in future generations the colour of coat in the blacks tends to a rusty dinginess, while the reds may develop into brindles. However, the first generation generally produces particularly clear, bright reds and really black blacks.

Miss M. Deck, the present Secretary of the Griffon Club has summed-up the Griffon character very concisely thus: 'They are hardy, adaptable and very affectionate. They can live a hard country life, with plenty of exercise and are excellent ratters. Or alternatively they can live in a flat in town without a great deal of exercise. They very soon take the noise and bustle in their stride. It is just a matter of how they are brought up. Sensibly reared and looked after they live to a good age.' So, really, what more can one want in an adaptable dog for these modern times? As the Griffon has never been a 'rave' breed, it has fortunately escaped all the disadvantages of over-popularity, when puppies are bred indiscriminately with only numbers in view which can be turned into easy money. Selective breeding has gone on more or less undisturbed in this breed, and the result is a type which breeds very consistently to form, without the attendant unsoundness which has unhappily come the way of quite a number of the more popular toy dogs.

5

Italian Greyhound

The Italian Greyhound is a petite replica of his larger brother, the Greyhound. He weighs between 6 and 8 lbs., and is therefore an ideal little fellow for the small house or flat. But he does need a certain amount of exercise if only to keep him warm. He loves nothing better than a chase on a common or in a park. He is fast with a delightful free action which enables him to turn rapidly while running.

He has so often been featured in paintings and portraits of the Tudor and Stuart periods. Shakespeare writes about Greyhounds in King Henry V though no doubt he was referring to the large variety. Undoubtedly the Italian Greyhound's big brother was a dog of the greatest antiquity, even mentioned in the Old Testament, and King Canute is reputed to have allowed only high-born gentlemen to own greyhounds since they were considered to be the cream of dogs.

The Italian Greyhound was known to be a great favourite of King Frederick II of Prussia, although even then he was much larger than we know him today.

It is said this larger type was inter-bred with Toy Terriers to diminish the size, and this policy was responsible for breeding out much of his grace and charm. Due to the careful, selective breeding which has been carried out over recent years, breeders have dealt with this problem and this little dog has won back his grace and elegance.

The Kennel Club Standard of the breed is short, concise and to the point. Here it is:

ITALIAN GREYHOUND

CHARACTERISTICS—High-stepping and free action.

GENERAL APPEARANCE—A miniature Greyhound, more slender in all proportions, and of ideal elegance and grace in shape, symmetry and action.

Head and Skull—Skull long, flat and narrow. Muzzle very fine. Nose dark in colour.

Eyes—Rather large, bright, and full of expression.

Ears—Rose-shaped, placed well back, soft and delicate.

Mouth—Teeth level.

Neck—Should be long and gracefully arched.

Forequarters—Shoulders long and sloping. Legs straight, well set under the shoulders; fine pasterns; small delicate bones.

Body—Chest deep and narrow. Back curved, and drooping at the hindquarters.

Hindquarters—Hocks well let down. Thighs muscular.

Feet—Long, hare-feet.

Tail—Rather long, fine, with low carriage.

Coat—Skin fine and supple. Hair, thin and glossy, like satin.

Colour—Recognised colours, all shades of fawn, white, cream, blue, black and fawn and white pied.

Weight and Size—The most desirable weight is from 6 to 8 lbs., and not exceeding 10 lbs.

Faults—Black or blue with tan markings, brindle.

When contemplating ownership of an Italian Greyhound, whether it is to be a puppy or an adult, there are several points to bear in mind. Of course, general healthiness and cleanliness which applies to all breeds, but in particular the Italian Greyhound should have a long, arched neck, curved back, and a long and fairly low-set tail. There is a wide variety of colour, but tan markings on black or blue dogs is not permissible. If the dog is desired as a companion, and not a show dog, it might be as well to choose one with not-too-slender legs, for there is no doubt that the Italian Greyhound (and amongst others the Chihuahua and the Toy Poodle) is sometimes prone to leg fractures. So a slightly more sturdy bone structure could be an advantage in all but the top show dog.

Grooming is comparatively simple. A moderately soft fibre hound glove, and a deal of polishing with either a velvet glove or silk handkerchief. But this little dog's coat must, above all, gleam and shine, and to achieve this gloss the dog must be a hundred per cent fit. Really sparkling good health will give a bright eye, and a shining coat. So the best of red meat, plenty of exercise, warm sleeping quarters—and don't forget that the little dog who is happy and well loved is going to have far more shine on his coat than the apprehensive, psychologically-disturbed little dog who lacks security and affection. So care for him and he will flourish and shine.

A word of warning here. The greatest possible care should be taken when grooming an Italian Greyhound to ensure that he is never left alone on the grooming table. So often an interruption occurs—the telephone rings, or there is a knock at the door—and the little dog jumps down from the table and the result is a fractured limb. Be sure either to put him on the floor or else to have a short lead and clip attached to the wall so that he cannot jump or fall.

The Italian Greyhound Championship Show is usually held in July of each year, and here are the details of the Challenge Certificate winners over the last five years:

THE ITALIAN GREYHOUND CLUB CHAMPIONSHIP SHOW

Year	*Dog Challenge Certificate*	*Bitch Challenge Certificate*	*Judge*
1964	Fleeting Fangio	Elsa of Ashgreen	Mrs. W. Barber
1965	Estrada Hermes	Charsfield Arrighini	Mrs. Barnard
1966	Estrada Marco of Velletri	Pussy Willow of Larchwood	Mrs. M. Garrish
1967	Odin Springinsfeld	Philtre Florena	Mrs. C. Lindhe
1968	Fleeting Flavius	Pussy Willow of Larchwood	Mrs. Morgan

The lovely little dog Odin of Springinsfeld was owned by

Mrs. Garrish and as well as being an English Champion, he had the double distinction of having obtained championship status in Austria. During the year 1967 he gained the dog challenge certificate at Crufts, Manchester, Glasgow, Three Counties, Blackpool and Hove, and was Best of Breed at three of these shows. The dog and bitch Challenge Certificate winners at Crufts over the past six years are given below:

CRUFTS CHAMPIONSHIP SHOW (ITALIAN GREYHOUNDS)

Year	*Dog Challenge Certificate*	*Bitch Challenge Certificate*	*Judge*
1964	Fleeting Fangio	Sheumac Silvertips	Mrs. Warner Hill
1965	Fleeting Fangio	Sheumac Silvertips	Mr. F. Cross
1966	Estrada Hermes	Sheumac Silvertips	Mrs. Hopwood
1967	Odin Springinsfeld	Philtre Florena	Mr. Fulwood
1968	Fleeting Flavius	Philtre Florena	Mrs. Barnard
1969	Juneric Red Admiral	Rusheen of Larchwood	Mrs. M. Garrish

Among the top winners who have done much for the breed, must be mentioned Mrs. Garrish (Fleeting), Mrs. Samuel (Sheumac), Mrs. Lewis (Philtre) and Messrs. Scholes and Street (Estrada).

The hat-trick was carried off by Mrs. Samuel when her lovely little bitch Sheumac Silvertips won Best Bitch for three years in succession at Crufts. Mrs. Lewis's Philtre Florena also brought Italian Greyhounds into the limelight by being judged Reserve Best in the Toy Group at Bath Championship Show in 1968, and Mrs. Hunter's Pussy Willow of Larchwood was Best Bitch at the Club Show in both 1966 and 1968. The Italian Greyhound Club held its first open show in 1961 and three years afterwards in 1964 was granted championship status at this show.

Registrations for the breed have been causing a little concern to breeders as they have been consistently dropping. Figures for 1967 were only 119 while in 1961 they were 198. While it is not a bad thing for a breed to have low registrations, for this usually means that what dogs there are have been very selectively bred and are therefore sound and true to type, but equally it may mean that a Club runs the risk of losing its allocation of Challenge Certificates, for C.C.'s are allotted in consideration of the number of registrations made by a particular breed. The total C.C.'s are then spread around the various Championship Shows. If there are not enough C.C.'s available then this means that the breed must lose championship status at one or several of the general championship shows and also at their own Club Show. So it behoves all Italian Greyhound breeders to register as many puppies as possible. At the moment Italian Greyhounds are thirteenth out of the 15 Toy breeds, being just below the King Charles Spaniels but rising one above the Japanese.

6

Japanese

A little dog not seen very often outside the show ring these days, which is surprising for he is small, easy to take about, not too onerous to groom and has the most delightful temperament—affectionate, loyal, full of spirit, with a great sense of fun. He bears a slight resemblance to the King Charles Spaniel, though he is a little smaller, and while both the head and the expression has something akin to the Pekingese, he is a far more petite little dog.

This breed is said to have gained recognition in Europe through Royal patronage for it appears that the Empress of China sent a breeding pair to the Empress of Germany in the late 1800's. However there are records which show that the Japanese was first exhibited in England in 1862. There is a long gap between that date and the first Japanese Championship Show which was held in 1968—over one hundred years later.

Here is the official Kennel Club Standard of the breed:

JAPANESE

GENERAL APPEARANCE—That of a lively, highly-bred little dog, of dainty appearance, smart, compact carriage, and profuse coat. These dogs should be essentially stylish in movement, lifting the feet high when in motion, carrying the tail (which is heavily feathered) proudly, curved or plumed over the back.

Head and Skull—Head should be large for size of dog, with broad skull, rounded in front; muzzle very short and wide and well-cushioned, i.e. the upper lips rounded on each side of the nostrils, which should be large and black, except in the case of red and white dogs, in which brown-coloured noses are as common as black ones.

Eyes—Should be large, dark, set far apart. It is desirable that the white shows in the inner corners, this gives the Japanese that characteristic look of astonishment (wrongly called 'squint') which should on no account be lost.

Ears—Should be small, set wide apart, and high on the dog's head, and carried slightly forward, V-shaped.

Mouth—Should be wide, neither undershot nor overshot.

Neck—Should not be too long.

Forequarters—The legs should be straight and the bone fine; well feathered to the feet.

Body—Should be squarely and compactly built, wide in chest, 'cobby' in shape. The length of the dog's body should be about its height.

Hindquarters—The legs should be straight and the bone fine; well feathered to the thighs behind.

Feet—Should be long and hare-shaped, also feathered.

Tail—Should be well plumed—carried proudly over the back.

Coat—Should be long, profuse and straight, free from curl or wave, and not too flat; it should have a tendency to stand out, more particularly at the frill, with profuse feathering on the tail and thighs.

Colour—The dogs should be either black and white or red and white, i.e. parti-coloured. The term red includes all shades of sable, brindle, lemon and orange, but the brighter and clearer the red the better. The white should be clear and the colour, whether black or red, should be evenly distributed as patches over the body, cheek and ears.

Weight and Size—When divided by weight, classes should be for under and over 7 lbs. In size they vary considerably, but the smaller they are the better, provided type and quality are not sacrificed.

Faults—'Flying' ears; narrow muzzle; too long a nose; tongue showing; light eyes; long back; dog being too near the ground through short legs; drooping tail; uneven markings; rounded short feet; wavy or curly coat; narrow chest; mouth undershot or overshot; weakness in hindquarters.

There are several points to avoid when buying a Japanese puppy or adult, apart from the general condition of health and cleanliness. A short-legged dog is not typical of the breed, for he is essentially a graceful, high-stepping little animal. Therefore, any Japanese which has a tendency to be 'low to ground' will suffer from a 'stumping' gait. Also the Japanese should be clearly marked with the colour evenly distributed. A wavy or curly coat is also undesirable, for this should be quite straight. Perhaps one of the most attractive traits of the Japanese, is his large dark eyes with the whites showing in the inner corners and giving an expression of astonishment. In the really well bred specimens, this expression is entrancing and most typical. Above all, he must be lively, high-stepping and always carry his heavily plumed tail well over his back.

To keep this little dog in tip-top condition, he needs quite constant grooming with a fairly soft bristle brush. Very little trimming is needed, and the comb should be used sparingly, except on the feathering of the fore-legs, the chest, the breeching at the back, and of course for the tail plume. This plume should be particularly profuse and carried well over the back, and should rather resemble a 'shower'. Care must be taken when grooming that the large and lustrous eyes are not damaged, and the runnels from the inside corners of the eyes should be kept clean with Vitacoat 'Diamondeye'. The coat must be straight but should also gleam, and thus polishing with a chammy leather is beneficial, but really, as with so many other breeds, careful and regular brushing is the keynote.

The Japanese Chin Club was founded in 1895, and Mr. Alfred De Rothschild did much to foster this breed in its early days. Now there are approximately 60 Club members, and Mrs. M. E. Searl is the present hard-working Secretary.

This breed has not yet found its way into the top twenty breeds, and perhaps because of that it has not been prostituted by the mass breeder who is attracted by popularity. Thus the Japanese has remained unspoilt over the years. The registrations at the Kennel Club remain, year by year, fairly steady, although there is a mild upward trend, for in 1958 only 58 were registered and the number has now climbed to around 130, but they are still in fourteenth position in the toy group of fifteen breeds.

At Crufts Show, moderate entries of Japanese are to be found, and usually the quality of the exhibits is excellent. Here are the Challenge Certificate Winners over the last six years.

CRUFTS CHAMPIONSHIP SHOW

Year	*Dog*	*Bitch*	*Judge*
1964	Momus of Riu Gu	Prince Kuchi Nashi	Mrs. Warner-Hill
1965	Momus of Riu Gu	Sandycuft Maiko of Riu Gu	Mr. Fred Cross
1966	Lamtoi Yo'san of Jongary	Vinovium Yum Yum	Mrs. Hopwood
1967	Nyorai of Riu Gu	Levanter Nagasaki	Mr. J. Allan
1968	Nyorai of Riu Gu	Michiko of Yevot	Mrs. N. Alexander
1969	Prince Mikasa of Camplane	Nimotsu of Riu Gu	Mr. W. G. Siggers

The First Japanese Chin Club Championship Show was held in Oxford in May 1968. The Challenge Certificate winners were:

Dog: Nyorai of Riu Gu *Bitch*: Michiko of Yevot
Best Puppy: Penwarne Jo Fu

The judge was Mr. George R. Down, and he made the dog C.C. winner the Best in Show. This first Club Championship Show was a great occasion and there were over 100 entries. The well-known Japanese breeder from Holland, Mrs. Van Douwe Moerkoert presented the fine collection of trophies to the winners.

Amongst those breeders who are never far from top honours are Mrs. Crauford of the Riu Gu Prefix (who is incidentally the President of the Club), Mrs. Jagger (Vinovium), and Mrs. Fearfield (Bowerhinton). Mrs. Tovey (Yevot) is another outstanding exhibitor for she won the Club Trophy for the Stud Dog of the Year with Mikami of Yevot for the second time, and her Michiko of Yevot was Best Bitch at the Club Championship Show, having gained her Junior Warrant in late 1966. Another wonderful honour came the way of the Japanese, for Mrs. Sharp's Prince Mikasa of Camplane was judged Reserve Best in the Toy Group at Crufts in 1969. A veritable little 'prince' who fairly sparkled round the ring, and was a great joy to watch.

The Secretary of the Japanese Chin Club, Mrs. M. E. Searl, has summed-up the Japanese as follows: 'A very gay, lively dog, that quickly adapts itself to the atmosphere of its home and its owners.' Certainly one has only to watch this enchanting little dog high-stepping round the ring, so very conscious of his own dignity, to realise that he is one of the most charming of the Toy breeds.

7

King Charles Spaniel

A delightful lap dog and yet sporting, fearless, and with a great wealth of affection for his owner—that is the King Charles Spaniel. A breed known in the days of Queen Elizabeth I and referred to in many of the early canine books as a 'comforter' or 'gentle spaniel' principally because he was much used by the ladies of the court to keep their feet warm under their voluminous skirts. They also had another function in life as they were frequently used as a means of luring the parasites from the same ladies on to their own bodies—not a very pleasant pastime for a dog! But it was really in the reigns of Charles I and II that these little dogs came into prominence, and it was Charles II who gave them the royal title. However, they did not much resemble the 'Charlie' of today for they were larger, had quite long noses and a flat head. Although considered to be an essentially English breed, the various colours appear to have emanated from the continent for the black and white variety is attributed to Holland, and the red and white to Italy.

A study of the Kennel Club's Standard of the breed gives a very clear picture:

KING CHARLES SPANIEL

GENERAL APPEARANCE—Compact and cobby, on refined lines, chest wide and deep, legs short and straight, back short and level. Tail well flagged, and not carried over the level of the back. Movement free, active and elegant.

Head and Skull—Skull massive in comparison to size,

Above: KING CHARLES SPANIELS. Huntglen King's Rhapsody of Oakridges, owned by Mrs. and Miss Harper. A well-coated specimen with plenty of feathering on legs, ears and tail. *Below:* KING CHARLES SPANIEL. This variety has the domed head and short nose, with well-defined stop. Compare the quite different head of the Cavalier King Charles Spaniel.

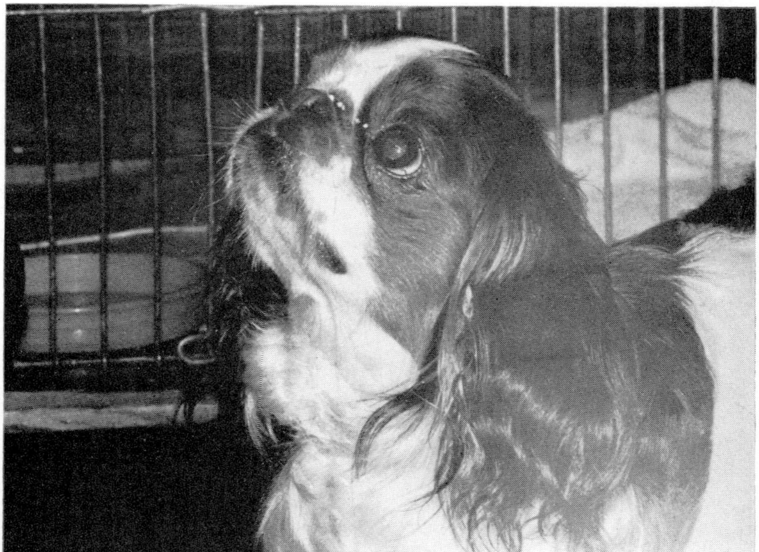

Above: CAVALIER KING CHARLES SPANIEL. Pargeter Dusty Answer, owned by Mrs. Keswick. A lovely dog demonstrating the short-coupled body and level top line, and possessing the silky coat which is free from curl. *Below:* CAVALIER KING CHARLES SPANIEL. Note the longer nose, well tapered muzzle and flat head of the Cavalier as compared with the King Charles.

well domed, and full over the eyes. Nose black with large wide open nostrils, very short and turned-up to meet the skull. The stop between skull and nose should be well defined. Jaw; muzzle square, wide, and deep and well turned-up, lower jaw wide, lips exactly meeting, giving a nice finish. The cheeks should not fall away under the eyes, but be well cushioned-up. A protruding tongue is objectionable but does not disqualify.

Eyes—Very large and dark, set wide apart, with eyelids block square to face line, and with pleasing expression.

Ears—Set on low, and to hang quite flat to cheeks, very long and well feathered.

Coat—Long, silky and straight, a slight wave allowed, not curly. The legs, ears and tail should be profusely feathered.

Colour—Black and Tan: A rich glossy black, with bright, mahogany tan markings, on muzzle, legs, chest, linings of ears, under tail, and spots over eyes. Tri-colour; Ground pearly white and well distributed black patches, brilliant tan markings on cheeks, linings of ears, under tail, and spots over the eyes. A wide white blaze between the eyes and up the forehead. Blenheim: A ground of pearly white with well distributed chestnut red patches. A wide clear blaze with the 'spot' in centre of skull. The 'spot' should be a clear chestnut red mark about the size of a sixpence in centre of skull. Ruby: Whole coloured, a rich chestnut red.

Weight and Size—The most desirable size is 8 to 14 lbs.

Faults—The presence of a few white hairs on the chest of a Black and Tan or Ruby is undesirable, but a white patch is a major fault.

There are four distinct varieties—the Blenheim evolved by the Duke of Marlborough at Blenheim Palace, hence the name, which is a lovely deep chestnut colour on a pearly white ground, and this variety has a wide clear blaze with the typical tan spot about the size of a sixpence in the centre of the skull. The Tricolour, often known as the Prince Charles

Spaniel, has black patches again on a pearly white ground, and also really bright tan markings on cheeks, linings of ears, under the tail and a spot over each eye. The Ruby is a rich chestnut colour all over. And finally the Black and Tan which has bright mahogany markings on a black ground as in the Tricolour but with no white, and in addition tan markings on legs and chest.

Grooming the 'Charlie' is a daily essential and a moderately soft-bristled human hair brush is suitable. A chromium-plated brass comb, fairly fine-toothed is suitable for finishing off, and to achieve that bright glossy sheen, polishing with a silk cloth or velvet glove is a good idea. Eyes, and below the eyes need daily inspection, and swabbing with Vitacoat 'Diamondeye' will clear away any extraneous matter caused by slight weeping. The King Charles can be bathed quite frequently and a good quality lanolin shampoo such as 'Chamoil' which has a high oil content or 'Olivite' which contains Dematol, and both prepared by Mr. Charles Warren of Vitacoat Ltd., are suitable and will bring up the coat to fine advantage, but for a show or a special occasion the shampooing should be carried out two or three days in advance to allow the natural oil to return to the coat, thus giving it plenty of gloss.

The King Charles Spaniel Club hold their annual show usually in May and the Challenge Certificate winners in both sexes and the names of the judges for the past five years are given on the opposite page.

Mr. Mannering and Mrs. Castle are very consistent winners with their Oakridges strain, with Mrs. Pennington (Tudorhurst) always well up in the awards. Mrs. Keswick's Pargeter Palamina has gained a number of C.C.'s as well as B.O.B. at Crufts.

The King Charles Spaniels do not alter a great deal in their total registrations for each year staying between 150 and 200, and have lain in 12th place in the Toy Breeds register over the years, sandwiched between the Miniature Pinschers and

THE KING CHARLES SPANIEL CHAMPIONSHIP SHOW

Year	*Dog Challenge Certificate*	*Bitch Challenge Certificate*	*Judge*
1964	Homehurst Merry Monarch	Laundra of Oakridges	Maj. Teager
1965	Bluerocks Jason of Jordans	Isobelle of Oakridges	Mrs. MacFarlane
1966	Goldendays Homehurst Gay Royal	Blueshadow Cresta	Miss D. Vincent
1967	Jerimiah of Jarrah	Claire of Vihurst	Mrs. P. Watson
1968	Charlies Rapture of Oakridges	Pargeter Palamina	Mr. Fullwood

And at Crufts some lovely specimens have won top honours in their breed:

CRUFTS CHAMPIONSHIP SHOW (KING CHARLES SPANIELS)

1964	Bluerocks Jason of Jordans	Isobelle of Oakridges	Mrs. W. Barber
1965	Bluerocks Jason of Jordans	Comforter of Oakridges	Mrs. F. Cross
1966	Karim of Ainsleyfield	Laundra of Oakridges	Mrs. Hopwood
1967	Tudorhurst Son of Monarch	Memories of Oakridges	Mrs. Warner-Hill
1968	Charlies Rapture of Oakridges	Pargeter Palamina	Mr. Fullwood
1969	Zepherine Clement	Memory of Oakridges	Mr. Warner-Hill

the Italian Greyhounds. They are quite a way behind their first cousins the Cavalier King Charles Spaniels in the popularity poll. It is extraordinary to remember that prior to 1928, 'Charlies' were the only type to be considered but by 1945 the Cavaliers had romped ahead.

These elegant, courtly little dogs are delightful in every way, and extremely aristocratic. Although there is quite a variation in size, they are on the whole smaller than the Cavaliers and this should appeal to those who feel the need for an affectionate, gay little dog who will give his whole heart to his owner. He is a dog for the connoisseur, and for one who likes something out of the ordinary.

8

Cavalier King Charles Spaniel

The history of this breed is perhaps more interesting than any other toy breed. Many people are not quite sure why some are called King Charles Spaniels and others Cavalier King Charles Spaniels—and what *is* the difference anyway?

Cavaliers were not recognised by the Kennel Club until 1945 and therefore one jumps to the false conclusion that these little dogs are comparatively new. But not a bit of it. The present day Cavalier King Charles has been revived from the days of the Stuarts and now resembles the little dogs so beloved of King Charles II; in fact it was this monarch who gave them the royal title. The King has so often been painted, accompanied by quite a horde of these dogs, and the famous diarist Pepys rather grumpily implied that the monarch spent more time over his Toy Spaniels than over the various pressing matters of State.

But as the years went on, the type of the dogs altered and in the Victorian era the nose became flattened, the skull domed with an accentuated stop between the eyes. A devotee of King Charles Spaniels, a certain Mr. Roswell Eldridge of New York, came over to England and was devastated to find that the 'old type' of Toy Spaniel had all but disappeared. He thereupon offered a prize of £25 each for the Best Dog and Best Bitch for 5 years at Crufts, and the definition in Crufts' Catalogue laid down that the dog or bitch was to be 'as shown in the picture of King Charles' II time with long face, no stop, flat skull not inclined to be domed, and with spot in the centre of the skull'. Needless to say, breeders did not think a great deal of this definition as they had spent many years evolving the squashed-in nose and domed skull with accentuated stop. However, a handful of really keen breeders started to re-develop the Toy Spaniel on Mr. Eldridge's definition, and in 1928 a Club was formed for this type. The problem of a suitable name then presented itself, for breeders did not want to lose the name 'King Charles', so after much heart-searching the name 'Cavalier King Charles Spaniel' was decided upon, and the required standard of breed points was drawn up. But there were still very few dogs of this type and the Kennel Club did not feel justified in granting a separate breed register until 17 years later. So until that time they were known as King Charles Spaniels (old type) until in 1945 the efforts of these selective and careful breeders were crowned with success, for the Kennel Club granted Challenge Certificates and thus championship status to the Cavalier King Charles Spaniel. Unfortunately, Mr. Roswell Eldridge died long before and therefore he did not have the satisfaction of knowing that this type of the little dogs he loved so much had gained recognition and risen to great popularity in England, being 4th in the popularity poll and only surpassed by the 'Rave' breeds of Yorkies, Pekes and Smooth Coated Chihuahuas, in that order.

Here is the Kennel Club Standard of the Breed:

CAVALIER KING CHARLES SPANIEL

GENERAL APPEARANCE—An active, graceful, well-balanced dog. Absolutely fearless and sporting in character and very gay and free in action.

Head and Skull—Head almost flat between the ears, without dome. Stop shallow; length from base of stop to tip about 1½ inches. Nostrils should be well developed and the pigment black. Muzzle well tapered. Lips well-covering but not hound-like. Face should be well filled out underneath the eyes. Any tendency to appear 'snipey' is undesirable.

Eyes—Large, dark and round, but not prominent. The eyes should be spaced well apart.

Ears—Long and set high, with plenty of feather.

Mouth—Level; scissor-bite preferred.

Neck—Moderate length—slightly arched.

Forequarters—Shoulders well laid back; legs moderate bone and straight.

Body—Short-coupled with plenty of spring of rib. Back level. Chest moderate leaving ample heart room.

Hindquarters—Legs with moderate bone; well-turned stifle—no tendency to cow or sickle hocks.

Feet—Compact, cushioned and well-feathered.

Tail—The docking of tails is optional. No more than one-third to be removed. The length of the tail should be in balance with the body.

Coat—Long, silky and free from curl. A slight wave is permissible. There should be plenty of feather.

Colour—Black and Tan—raven black with tan markings above eyes, on cheeks, inside ears, on chest, legs and underside of tail. Tan should be bright. Ruby—whole-coloured rich red. Blenheim—rich chestnut markings well broken-up on a pearly-white ground. The markings should be evenly divided on the head, leaving room between the ears for the much valued lozenge mark or spot (a unique characteristic of the breed). Tri-colour—Black and white, well spaced and broken-up, with tan markings over the eyes, on cheeks, inside ears, inside legs and on underside of tail. Black and white—Permissible but not desirable.

Weight and Size—Weight: 12 to 18 lbs. A small well-balanced dog, well between these weights is desirable.

Faults—Light eyes. Undershot and crooked mouths and pig jaws. White marks on whole coloured specimens. Coarseness of type. Putty noses. Flesh marks. Nervousness.

A very great attribute of the Cavalier is that he is fearless and sporting and not really in any way a lap-dog. Also he should be gay and well dispositioned. Breeders have been singularly selective in their breeding programmes to ensure that this sweet nature should be one of the highlights of this little dog's make-up. So when choosing a puppy a prospective owner can be reasonably sure he will get a dog with a good temperament. When buying a puppy, level mouths with strong, even teeth should be looked for. There are several colours, i.e., Black and Tan, Ruby, Blenheim which is a white ground with chestnut markings, or the Tricolour, black, white, and tan, and if buying a whole-coloured puppy be sure there are no white markings as these are considered definite faults. Also choose a puppy with a really black nose as liver or flesh-coloured noses are not desirable.

The tail may be docked or left to its natural length. This is completely optional on the part of the breeder and is one of the few breeds in which that is so.

As regards grooming, a daily brushing with a good quality not-too-hard brush, possibly a 'Mason Pearson' or similar, and a combing with a chromium-plated brass comb is necessary. The coat must be silky and straight, therefore a good gloss is indicated, and to this end, polishing with a silk handkerchief or velvet glove puts a lovely sheen on the coat.

The Cavalier breeders, very much to their credit, are extremely anxious that their precious breed should not fall into the hands of accomplished handlers, which might mean losing their particular characteristics. Thus they decided that there should be no stripping or use of scissors, so that there was no danger of the breed becoming artificially altered to achieve special good points. In one or two of the breeds which need tremendous skill and artistry, it is well-nigh impossible for the novice to enter the ring at all with any hope of winning. But not so with the Cavalier. It is a natural breed, and Cavalier owners mean to keep it that way, and they are adamant in encouraging the breeders of healthy, natural dogs who can be shown by anyone. And they have certainly achieved their aim. When a breed is really popular there is a great risk that indiscriminate breeding will take place because the demand exceeds the supply. Thus the quality goes down, and so often exaggerated trimming is carried out to cover up many of the appalling faults which lie hidden under fabulous coats 'shaped' to perfection. How wise the Cavalier people have been to scotch that! To possess a shining coat, bright eyes and fearless disposition the Cavalier puppy must be reared on good food, be kept in clean surroundings, have the mind-stimulation of living with its owner and not be restricted both mentally and physically in a kennel, and above all he must be psychologically secure and unworried in his everyday life. Therefore be sure that all the necessary chores of grooming, training, etc., are made as enjoyable as possible, and not occasions of dread and fearful anticipation.

The popularity of this breed continues to rise, and each year more and more Cavaliers are registered. In 1954, the number was 794 and ten years later it was 2,352 against a mere 170 for the King Charles Spaniel. In 1966 they entered the Top Twenty of All Breeds, in 18th place, the only other Toy Breeds in this list being Yorkshire Terriers in 5th place, Pekingese in 12th place and Smooth Chihuahuas, just topping them in 17th place by less than 100 registrations.

The Cavalier King Charles Spaniel Club usually hold their Club Championship Show in March or April each year, and the Challenge Certificate winners at this show over the past five years are given overleaf.

Cavaliers have certainly distinguished themselves in the show-ring against other breeds, for in 1963 Mrs. Cryer's Amelia of Laguna was judged Best Toy at Crufts and then Best Bitch all breeds on the first day, while Mrs. Pitt's Sugar Crisp of Ttiweh was judged Best in Show all breeds at a New Zealand Championship Show. In 1965 Vairire Duchess Xenia of Santander, owned by Mrs. Taylor, was the winner of the Toy Group at Windsor while more recently Lady Forwood's Archie McMuck of Eyeworth won the Puppy Stakes at Bath Championship Show and Mrs. Percival's Bowstones Victoria of Little Breach was judged Reserve Best Toy at Windsor Championship Show.

CAVALIER KING CHARLES SPANIEL CLUB CHAMPIONSHIP SHOW

Year	*Dog*	*Bitch*	*Judge*
1964	Minshang Danby	Millstone Barings Margareta	Miss B. Sadler
1965	Heatherside Perry	Vairire Duchess Xenia of Santander	Mrs. H. Warner-Hill
1966	Crisdig Merry Matelot	Harriet of Hillbarn	Mrs. I. J. Green
1967	Pargeter McBounce	Pargeter Trelawney	Mr. F. Cross
1968	Pargeter Dusty Answer	Carmen o'Cockpen	Mrs. E. Pilkington

There is always an excellent entry at Crufts each year and in 1969 Cavaliers were the biggest Toy Entry. Here are the C.C. winners and names of the judges over the last six years:

CRUFTS CHAMPIONSHIP SHOW (CAVALIERS)

1964	Edward of Knightlow	Pargeter Melissa	Mrs. J. Bowdler
1965	Timja Clarinet	Mimi of Eyeworth	Mrs. H. Warner-Hill
1966	Eyeza Crisdig Pip	Startime of Statfold	Mr. J. H. Braddon
1967	Crisdig Harlequin	Josephine of Blagreaves	Mrs. E. Pilkington
1968	Budougol Bankrupt	McGoogans Molly Malone	Lady Forwood
1969	Vairire Osiris	Piccola of Crustadele	Miss P. Turle

Miss Douglas's Vairire Osiris showed superbly at the West of England Cavalier Club Championship Show, and carried off the award of Best in Show, following this with the distinction of Best of Breed at Crufts in 1969.

Amongst the early pioneers of the Cavaliers, all of whom have done so much to foster the old type, are Mrs. Amice Pitt (Ttiweh), Mrs. Jennings (Plantation), Mrs. Daphne Murray (Crustadele), Mrs. Rackham, and Miss Mostyn-Walker who bred the celebrated dog Ann's Son. As will be seen by the foregoing show winners, Mrs. Keswick of Pargeter prefix, Mrs. Burgess (Crisdig) and Mrs. Garratley (Statfold) are never far from the top.

The Cavalier King Charles Spaniel Club now has over 400 members. They are a most keen and lively body of people, and an excellent year book is published. In 1968 they celebrated their Jubilee year, and without any doubt this Club must take top place for the help and encouragement it gives to all owners and prospective owners of this lovely breed.

The Secretary of the Club, Mrs. Pamela Freedman sums up the Cavalier King Charles Spaniel very neatly thus: 'A loving and faithful disposition but inclined to greediness and luxury, if available. Adapts well to cold Swedish winters and hot Australian summers.'

Certainly one of the nicest, best mannered dogs on the Toy register. One almost expects him to sweep-off his finely plumed hat and give one a deep, courtly bow!

9

Maltese

Again, the history of this gay, little white breed is difficult to trace as there seems to be much divergence of opinion as to which was the true country of origin. It appears to be established however that the Maltese is one of the original French toy breeds. Only four are now recognised, the remaining three being the Bolognese, the Havanese, and the Tenerife Dog. But the Maltese is the only one recognised in England with a standard of its own at the Kennel Club. Certainly, the Maltese is one of the most ancient breeds of dogs whose history goes back further than any other. Strabo, writing in A.D. 25 said there was a town in Sicily called Melita where beautiful little dogs called *Canis Melitei* were to be found but equally Stanley Dangerfield tells us it is known that at this time Publius, the Roman Governor of Malta, owned a Maltese called 'Issa'. They were particular favourites of ladies who carried them about in the bosoms of their dresses and allowed them to sleep in their beds, but it must be realised that in their original days these little dogs were very little bigger than ferrets. Coming up to our own time, breeders have attempted to import new stock direct from Malta. However, they have found not small toy dogs but enormous dogs who were no use at all for improving the Maltese as we know it. Luckily, smaller specimens were found in other Continental countries which have served this purpose.

The Maltese really has had quite a chequered career and has often been on the brink of extinction. Landseer, the great animal artist hurriedly painted one of these little white dogs in the early 1800's because he said it was the last of its race. However, the Maltese was not to be disposed of like this and rose again towards the middle of that century, being quite a frequent exhibit at the early dog shows, and again because of his size no doubt became a great ladies' pet. Possibly the worst set-back experienced by this breed was during the First World War when they all but faded into complete obscurity, but again they just survived, and now over 300 are registered at the Kennel Club each year. Being white they are most photogenic, and also have modelled for many artists, not least of course the famous Sir Joshua Reynolds who portrayed a Maltese in the painting of Nellie O'Brien.

The Standard lays down that the Maltese must be lively and alert. Certainly he is a great hunter of the smaller types of rodent, and loves nothing better than to hunt along a hedgerow after field-mice and voles, much to the detriment of his lovely coat. But of course, this breed was originally a terrier and so this type of pastime comes quite naturally to him. Perhaps one of the greatest attributes of this little dog is his great sense of humour and fun. He is literally always ready to join in a joke, and his particularly sweet temper never lets him take umbrage at anything.

Here is the Standard of the breed as laid down by the Kennel Club.

MALTESE

CHARACTERISTICS—Sweet tempered and very intelligent.

GENERAL APPEARANCE—Should be smart, lively and alert. The action must be free, without extended weaving.

Head and Skull—From stop to centre of skull (centre between forepart of ears) and stop to tip of nose should be equally balanced. Stop should be defined. Nose should be pure black.

Eyes—Should be dark brown, with black eye-rims, set in centre cheeks and not bulging.

Ears—Should be long and well feathered and hanging close to the side of the head, the hair to be mingled with the coat at the shoulders.

Mouth—Level or scissor bite with teeth even.

Neck—Of medium length—set on well sloped shoulders.

Forequarters—Legs should be short and straight. Shoulders well sloped.

Body—Should be in every way well balanced and essentially short and cobby, with good rib spring and the back should be straight from the tip of the shoulders to the tail.

Hindquarters—Legs should be short and nicely angulated.

Feet—Should be round and the pads of the feet should be black.

Tail—Should be well arched over the back and feathered.

Coat—Should be good length, but not impeding action, of silky texture, not in any way woolly and should be straight. It should not be crimped and there should be no woolly undercoat.

Colour—Pure white, but slight lemon markings should not penalise.

Size—Not over 10 inches from ground to top of shoulder.

Faults—Bad mouth, over or undershot; gay tail; curly or woolly coat; brown nose; pink eye-rims; unsound in any way.

The grooming of the Maltese is not easy, and if he is to look smart and invariably chic a great deal of time must be spent on his coat. After he has been bathed, and to keep him in tip-top condition this can be carried out quite often, his coat should shine like driven snow. The hair is long, though not long enough for him to trip over it like the Yorkie, and it should be really silky, hence the desired shine. The hair must also be straight and by no means crimped, and above all tendency to woolliness or woolly undercoat is quite wrong. A soft bristle brush should be used, and the hair parted straight down the middle of the back from neck to root of tail, and then brushed carefully down each side. The hair should be trimmed so that it is just clear of the floor. The hair on the head can be gathered into a top knot and tied with ribbon after the style of the poodle top knot, but equally the hair can be divided into a tress on each side of the head, and these tresses plaited into two pig-tails, the ends being neatly tied with ribbon. Certainly the Maltese is one of the most profusely, densely-coated of dogs. The eyes should be kept clean, and any tendency to ugly staining caused by weeping can be treated by regular swabbing with Vitacoat 'Diamond-Eye' which is quite excellent. A lanolin shampoo is called for, and 'Bleufonce De Luxe' or 'Chamoil' seem to suit these dogs' coats admirably, with a final tonic rinse such as 'Cream Coat Corrector', all prepared by Vitacoat Ltd.

Certainly, to keep this breed always immaculate and with his coat always long enough, yet dense and not wispy is a real work of art, and if you intend to show this breed you should have specialised knowledge and not take on the task too lightly. As a pet, such perfection is possibly not so necessary and as a result the companion Maltese can enjoy complete freedom but obviously will not have such a fabulous coat. He certainly is a marvellous companion and very single minded in his devotion to his owner.

The Maltese is about midway down the Popularity Poll of the 15 Toy breeds, having stayed in 10th place for many, many years. Registration figures have moved up from just under 200 in the early 1950's to around 340 at the present time, so the breed is obviously making headway. The Annual Championship Show is usually held in April, and the Challenge Certificate winners in both sexes at this Show over the last three years are given overleaf.

From the results it will be seen that of the outstanding breeders who have had considerable success Mrs. Lewin (Ellwin), Miss White (Vicbrita) and Mrs. Collins (Zurvic) are seldom far from the top.

In 1968, spectacular wins have come the way of Mrs. Lewin's splendid little bitch Ellwin Victoriana, for she was

THE MALTESE CLUB CHAMPIONSHIP SHOW

Year	*Dog Challenge Certificate*	*Bitch Challenge Certificate*	*Judge*
1966	Immacula Top O' the Poll	Triogen Toppet	Mrs. Brierley (Dogs) Miss M. Wild (Bitches)
1967	Margretwoods Alyssum	Ellwin Melusine	Mrs. Roberts
1968	Cusenier of Zurvic	Ellwin Victoriana	Mrs. E. V. Hogg

And here are the top Maltese at Crufts over the last six years:

CRUFTS CHAMPIONSHIP SHOW (MALTESE)

1964	Vicbrita Fidelity	Shenala Festoon	Miss M. Wild
1965	Vicbrita Fidelity	Ellwin Marietta	Mrs. M. Crook
1966	Martini of Zurvic	Vicbrita Delight	Mr. Fullwood
1967	Ellwin Pippelo	Vicbrita Petit Point	Mr. Siggers
1968	Vicbrita Tobias	Ellwin Victoriana	Mrs. W-Hill
1969	Cusenier of Zurvic	Saumarez Baa Baa	Mrs. Roberts

Above: MALTESE. Vibrita Tobias, owned by Miss White. A lovely specimen with a wealth of flowing coat, who has been right at the top of his breed for some time. *Below:* MALTESE. His profuse and well-cared for coat is carefully protected when he is not in the show ring.

Above: MINIATURE PINSCHER. Birling Wawocan Constellation, owned by Mr. Hamilton Renwick. A splendid example of this breed, and the winner of 26 Challenge Certificates, as well as Reserve Best Toy at Crufts, 1967. *Below:* MINIATURE PINSCHER. Birling Bright Star, owned by Mr. Hamilton Renwick. Note the stance of this lovely dog, with level top line and fine alert expression.

judged Reserve Best in Show on the first day of Leicester Championship Show, was best in Toy group at Crufts, Peterborough and Bournemouth Championship Shows, going on to Best Opposite Sex in Show at the latter show. Truly a magnificent little white lady. Mrs. White's Vicbrita Tobias has also achieved some splendid wins for he was judged Best Toy Dog at both Birmingham National and the City of Birmingham Championship Shows, while the same owner's Vicbrita Consul won the Puppy Stakes at both Leicester and the City of Birmingham Championship Shows. He is as boldly masculine as Victoriana is sweetly feminine. In 1968, out of the twenty-eight available Challenge Certificates won by Maltese, no less than twenty-two went to Maltese owning one or both Vicbrita parents.

The secretaryship of the Maltese Club has been taken over by Mrs. Collins of Zurs, Hill Brown, Liss, in Hampshire. The Club was founded in 1934 and now has over 100 members. In the early days Mrs. M. Roberts, Miss M. Neame, and also the President of the Club Miss Worthington all did sterling work for the Maltese.

In these days, when the tiny dog is much sought after, certainly the little Maltese could be an excellent choice. He should not measure more than 10″ at the shoulder, and weigh a mere four to nine pounds, and his really charming personality is one of his greatest assets. Mrs. C. M. Hunter of the famous Gissing Kennel of Maltese has summed-up the character of this breed for the authors admirably. She says, 'The Maltese is adaptable to any life, provided he is treated as a member of the family. He needs much human love. He has a wonderful character, and is devoted and fearless. Throughout their history, Maltese have been noted for their powers of easing pain and at times of healing it.'

Mrs. Hunter has been secretary of the Maltese Club for the past 15 years but now to the loss of the Maltese world, has left England with her little dogs to take up residence in Portugal where she hopes to find the sun!

10

Miniature Pinscher

The Miniature Pinscher is a most attractive little dog with great sporting interests and plenty of courage and spirit. Originally this breed came from Germany where it was known as the Reh Pinscher, but it is a very old breed which has connections with Peat country, where Pinschers were kept quite extensively as stable dogs or ratters. Separate classes were first put on for the Miniature Pinscher in Berlin in 1888, and the first Miniature Pinscher Club was formed in 1895. Although a few of these tiny terrier-like dogs were seen in England in the first half of the century, there were only a handful of them until the mid-1960's. Since then they have enjoyed rather more popularity.

Here is the official Standard of the breed:

MINIATURE PINSCHER

GENERAL APPEARANCE—The Miniature Pinscher is structurally a well balanced, sturdy, compact, elegant, short-coupled, smooth-coated toy dog. He is naturally well groomed, proud, vigorous and alert. The natural characteristic traits which identify him from other toy dogs are his precise Hackney gait, his fearless animation, complete self-possession and his spirited presence.

Head and Skull—Rather more elongated than short and round. Narrow and without conspicuous cheek formation. In correct proportion to the body. The skull should appear flat when viewed from the front. The muzzle must be rather strong and proportionate to the skull. The nose well formed, black only with the exception of livers and blues, which may have a self-coloured nose.

Eyes—Fitting well into the face. Neither too full nor round, neither too little nor slanting. Black or nearly black.

Ears—Must be set on high, as small as possible, erect or dropped.

Mouth—Scissors bite.

Neck—Strong yet graceful. Slightly arched. Well fitted into the shoulders. Free from throatiness.

Forequarters—Forechest well developed and full, moderately broad, shoulders clean, sloping with moderate angulation. Co-ordinated to permit the true action of the Hackney pony.

Body—To be square, back line straight, sloping slightly towards the rear. Belly moderately tucked-up. Ribs well sprung, deep rather than barrelled. Viewed from the top, slightly wedge-shaped.

Hindquarters—Should be parallel to each other and wide enough apart to fit in with a properly built body. The hindquarters should be well developed and muscular with a good sweep of stifle and their hocks turning neither in nor out.

Feet—Legs straight, medium bone. Feet cat-like, elbows close to body. Nails dark.

Tail—A continuation of the top-line carried a little high and docked short.

Coat—Smooth, hard and short. Straight and lustrous. Closely adhering to and uniformly covering the body.

Colour—Black, blue, chocolate with sharply defined tan markings on cheeks, lips, lower jaw, throat, twin spots above eyes and chest, lower half of fore-legs, inside of hindlegs and vent region, lower portion of hocks and feet. All the above colours should have black pencilling on toes with no thumb marks. Solid red of various shades. Slight white on chest is permissible but undesirable.

Height—The height to range from 10 to 12 inches at the withers.

As will be seen from the foregoing, one of the great delights of the Miniature Pinscher is his lovely gait which should resemble that of a prancing Hackney pony. There are a variety of colours—black, blue, chocolate, but all with the typical tan markings. Unlike the English Toy Terrier (Black and Tan) there must however, be no black thumb marks above the toes. Ears may be pricked or dropped, and the tail must be docked short.

Miniature Pinschers will benefit considerably if the 'Charbon' treatment is used as an alternative means to bathing. This type of shampooing is described fully in the chapter dealing with Chihuahuas.

Grooming of the Miniature Pinscher is not onerous, and lies mostly in achieving a really good sheen or gloss on the hair. A fibre hound glove is excellent for this particular coat, with final brisk polishing with a piece of silk or a velvet glove.

The Miniature Pinscher Club usually hold their annual Championship Show during mid-summer, and the dog and bitch Challenge Certificate winners at that show over the past five years together with the names of the judges are given on the opposite page.

Undoubtedly, Mr. Hamilton-Renwick must be acclaimed as the leading Miniature Pinscher breeder and exhibitor in this country, for he certainly does appear to hold the formula in both spheres. His great little dog Birling Bright Star can not only claim many Toy Group wins, among them Windsor, the West of England Ladies' Kennel Society, Hove and Dumfries, also Reserve Best in Show on the first day at the W.E.L.K.S., and Best in Show at the Miniature Pinscher Club Championship Show, but he is the son of that equally outstanding dog Birling Wawocan Constellation who performed the hat-trick at the Club Championship Show by winning Best in Show for 3 years in succession, and Best of Breed at Crufts for three years, and has won over 25 Challenge Certificates. Constellation is also the sire of Birling

THE MINIATURE PINSCHER CLUB CHAMPIONSHIP SHOW

Year	*Dog Challenge Certificate*	*Bitch Challenge Certificate*	*Judge*
1964	Birling Wawocan Constellation	Shumah Parasol	Mrs. Lennox
1965	Birling Wawocan Constellation	Tannoir Airs 'n Graces	Miss Humphries
1966	Birling Wawocan Constellation	Shumah Alkara Cheetah	Mr. J. Stott
1967	Toykokep Music Man	Shumah Firebird	Mrs. Walker
1968	Birling Bright Star	Anjondro Altro	Mr. Dawson

And here are the equivalent wins for Crufts for the last six years:

CRUFTS CHAMPIONSHIP SHOW (MINIATURE PINSCHERS)

1964	Birling Wawocan Constellation	Little Squib	Mrs. Warner-Hill
1965	Birling Wawocan Constellation	Birling Painted Lady	Mr. Moody
1966	Duiker Sykes	Birling Painted Lady	Mrs. W. Barber
1967	Birling Wawocan Constellation	Shumah Firebird	Mrs. Race
1968	Birling Bright Star	Bragan Queen Bee	Mrs. Curnow
1969	Birling Bright Star	Tannoir Hy Ness	Mr. Warner-Hill

Painted Lady, holder of over 20 Challenge Certificates. Other breeders and exhibitors who are seldom far away when the Challenge Certificates are being awarded are Miss Humphries (Shuman), Mrs. Langley with Toykokep Music Man, and Mrs. Walker (Tannoir).

Miniature Pinschers have occupied eleventh place in the Toy Breeds Register for many years now, being just above the King Charles Spaniel and below the Maltese. Registration numbers have remained roughly between 150 and 250 over the last ten years, but seem to be just slightly on the increase of late.

Certainly, one could look at many other breeds and realise that the Miniature Pinscher has much to offer as the perfect companion. He is so very self-possessed and full of life, and has such abundant courage. If you are looking for a dog who needs only very little attention in the matter of grooming, has the intelligence to learn quickly the lessons of life, who is small and therefore able to fit snugly into the needs of our modern everyday life, then consider well all the advantages a Miniature Pinscher has to offer.

11

Papillon

Perhaps one of the daintiest and prettiest of all the Toy breeds, the Papillon is said to have originated in Mexico, as other large-eared breeds such as the Chihuahua and Mexican hairless dogs have done. They then made their way to Belgium with which country they are more generally associated. As their name implies, they are also known as the Butterfly dogs, and undoubtedly the huge ears do resemble a butterfly with wide-spread wings. These ears are certainly his crowning glory for they are heavily fringed with long silky hair, and the tips of the ears point outwards giving the alert, quizzical look so typical of this breed. Usually the ears are pricked, but there is also a drop-eared variety called Epagneuls Nains but these are not seen so often in England. Oddly enough, this enchanting little dog does not enjoy a great popularity with the general public, although to anyone who has had the privilege of owning or breeding Papillons they are unanimously agreed that there is no sweeter little dog, nor one with more pleasant manners.

Here is the official Standard of the Breed as laid down by the Kennel Club, and it will be seen that a considerable amount of detail as to faults is laid down. This will greatly help the amateur to choose wisely when buying either a puppy or an adult, providing this official Standard is well studied before purchase.

PAPILLON

GENERAL APPEARANCE—This dainty, balanced little toy dog

should have an attractive head, an alert bearing and an intelligent and lively expression. Movement should be sound, light and free and not cramped or restricted in any way.

Head and Skull—The skull slightly rounded between the ears, the muzzle finely pointed and abruptly thinner than the skull accentuating the stop which should be well defined. Length from tip of the nose to the stop approximately a third length of the head. Nose should be black.

Faults—Muzzle over long or coarse. Skull flat or apple-shaped. Nose other than black.

Eyes—Of medium size, rounded, dark in colour, placed rather low in the head and should not bulge.

Faults—Eyes light in colour, too small or too large or protruding.

Ears—The ears should be large with rounded tips, heavily fringed, set towards the back of the head far enough apart to show the slightly rounded shape of the skull. The ears must be completely erect or dropped. When the ears are erect they must be carried obliquely like the spread wings of a butterfly, therefore the name, Papillon. When the ears are dropped they must be completely dropped, and thus type is known as the Phalene (moth).

Faults—Semi-erect or not fully dropped, small, sharply pointed or set too close together.

Mouth—Scissor bite, upper teeth fitting close over lower. The lips thin and tight.

Faults—Over- or undershot to the extent that the incisors do not touch at all. Wry mouth.

Neck—Of medium length.

Forequarters—Shoulders well developed and sloping back. Chest rather deep. Forelegs straight and slender and fine boned.

Faults—Shoulders straight. Out at elbow.

Body—Level topline. The body should have plenty of length, well formed with well sprung ribs, good length of loin which must not be weak, with slightly arched belly.

Above: PAPILLON. Amberbrook Vega, owned by Mrs. Maynard. Here one sees the very large and heavily fringed ears which suggest an open-winged butterfly. A sweet natured little dog with a lovely expression. *Below:* PAPILLON. An abundantly coated little dog with the back parts of front legs, tail and thighs well feathered. A tail which is set on high, curving over the back with a fine plume.

Above: PEKINGESE. Siangyang Puff Puff, owned by Mrs. White. A gay young puppy waiting to go into the ring, having qualified for entry at Crufts. *Below:* PEKINGESE. This photograph shows the massive head and broad skull, the short nose and the attractive black mask.

Above: POMERANIAN. Mosey the Menace of Vernlil, owned by Mrs. Weinert. An intelligent little toy dog with the correct foxy expression, small erect ears, and with a profuse outstanding coat. He reached championship status when barely out of puppyhood. *Below:* POMERANIAN. A short coupled little dog, with the well-carried tail, and typically elegant hocks and feet.

Above: PUG. Muchmor Buff Orpington of Pyebeta, owned by Mrs. Purcell. The wrinkles on the face are large and deep, and the head massive with the typical eyes, which are soft and solicitous in expression. The small ear is like black velvet. *Below:* PUG. A splendid example of this breed, showing the square, cobby body, strong straight legs, with the tightly curled tail.

Faults—Topline roached, dipped or cobby. Legs malformed and crooked, cow-hocked, too long or too short. Stifles straight, coupled with weak hindquarters.

Hindquarters—Well developed, good turn of stifle. Legs when viewed from behind, should be parallel. Dew claws on the hind legs must be removed.

Feet—Fine and fairly long as in the hare. The tufts of hair between the toes extending far beyond them.

Tail—Long and well fringed, set on high, arched over the back with fringes falling to the side to form the plume.

Faults—Tail unduly short, too low set.

Coat—Should be abundant, (flowing) but without undercoat, long, fine, silky, falling flat on back and sides forming a profuse frill on the chest, short and close on the skull, muzzle and front part of the legs. Back part of the front legs to pasterns, tail and thighs covered with long hair.

Faults—Harsh, curly or stand-off coat.

Colour—White with patches which may be any colour except liver. A tricolour must be black and white with tan spots over the eyes, tan inside ears and under root of tail and on cheeks. The head marking should be symmetrical about a white, narrow, clearly defined blaze.

Size—The ideal height at the withers from 8 to 11 ins. The dog will appear to be slightly longer than high when properly furnished with ruff and hind fringes.

Faults—Muzzle over long or coarse. Skull flat or apple-shaped. Nose other than black. Eyes light in colour, too small or too large or protruding. Ears semi-erect or not fully dropped, small, sharply pointed or set too close together. Mouth over or undershot to the extent that the incisors do not touch at all. Wry mouth. Shoulders straight. Out at elbow. Topline roached, dipped or cobby. Legs malformed and crooked, cow hocked, too long or too short. Stifles straight, coupled with weak hindquarters. Tail unduly short, too low set. Harsh, curly or stand-off coat.

To keep the Papillon in good fettle, he needs regular daily grooming with a long, not-too-hard bristle brush. A medium-toothed comb should be used for the long haired parts. The hair is silky and straight, and should lie flat on sides and back, and therefore should shine with healthy gloss. The coat should never be fluffy or stand out from the body as does the Pomeranian's coat. Next to the ears, the glorious tail plume is a great beauty and this should be profusely feathered, falling to one side over the back. Practically no trimming is carried out, just a tidying of any ragged ends. He needs careful and regular shampooing with a good quality lanolin shampoo such as 'Bleu-Fonce de Luxe', with a special rinse with 'Cream Coat Corrector', both prepared by Vitacoat Ltd., of Croydon, Surrey. Bathing should be carried out a day or two before any special date to allow the natural oil to return to the coat. Polishing with the bare hand or a silk handkerchief will add the desired sheen to the coat.

When buying a 'Pap' pup, special attention should be given to a dark nose and eye. A liver or pink coloured nose is a fault and rather unsightly. Oddly enough the Papillon should *not* be too short in back, which is the opposite of most breeds, therefore a longer back to accommodate the tail plume, and a good level topline. Colour is also important, and any dog which is all one colour, or all black and tan, is frowned upon. So when choosing a puppy the ideal is a white ground with tan markings evenly on head, and tan patches on body. Equally, as the Standard lays down, tri-colour is also desirable. But in each case a well defined white blaze must appear on the head above the eyes.

Papillons have remained steadily in 7th place in the Toy breeds register for many years, although registrations have almost doubled from around 300 to 600 over the years. They have not so far aspired to inclusion in the top twenty all-breed list.

The Papillon Club was founded in 1923, and Mrs. Helen

Lake (Otter), Madame Oosterveen (Monamie) and Mrs. Williams (Ardna) all did a great deal to foster this fascinating breed in its early days. The Club now has over 300 members, and a most interesting and informative Year Book is published every five years. The most recent edition was published in 1968, and costs 12/6d.

The Club holds its Championship Show usually in March, and the winners of the Challenge Certificates for both dogs and bitches at this show over the past five years, together with the names of the judges officiating are given overleaf.

Amongst those usually to be seen well at the top in the show ring are Mr. and Mrs. Blayney (Palmoza), Mrs. Harris (Stouravon), Mrs. Henderson (Inverdon), Mrs. McGregor-Cheers (Baluch), Mrs. Moss-Blundell (Barberie) and Mr. and Mrs. Russell-Roberts (Picaroon). Mr. and Mrs. Ratigan had considerable success with their Rosabunda of Costa Brava having been judged Best Toy Bitch at Birmingham National Championship Show, and also Best Bitch in the Toy Group at the City of Birmingham Championship Show. Mrs. McGregor-Cheers has for the last two years carried-off the dog Challenge Certificate with Baluch Little Shenandoah at both the Club Show and Crufts. Mrs. Foreman has combined beauty with obedience with her Bordercot Papillons, for in addition to generations of Challenge Certificate winners, both her Bordercot Gem and Bordercot Georgie have gained their C D ex in the obedience field.

Certainly a Papillon would be an excellent choice for anyone wanting a hardy toy dog, carrying with it fearlessness of other breeds, inquisitiveness, and mischievousness, and to cap it all pure elegance, allied with a sweet nature. Miss Waud, secretary of the Papillon Club sums up the breed like this: 'A dainty, small toy dog with long, flowing coat, heavily-fringed ears like the open wings of a butterfly. A lively, intelligent little dog, generally sweet-tempered and adaptable. Not particularly suited for rough romps with children, but a loyal and delightful companion for the older

THE PAPILLON CLUB CHAMPIONSHIP SHOW

Year	*Dog Challenge Certificate*	*Bitch Challenge Certificate*	*Judge*
1964	Picaroon Pan	Ringlands Red Link	Mrs. E. Benson
1965	Stouravon Greenjackets Mariner	Winch Could Be	Mr. Leo Wilson
1966	Holmlea Gay Harry	Picaroon Crepes D'Enfer	Mr. L. Ratigan
1967	Baluch Little Shenandoah	Inverdon Leila	Mr. F. Cross
1968	Baluch Little Shenandoah	Inverdon Leila	Mr. H. Benson

And here are similar details for Crufts:

CRUFTS CHAMPIONSHIP SHOW (PAPILLONS)

1964	Wychdale Pierre	Thingden Little Mo	Mrs. G. A. Swann
1965	Stouravon Elegant Mink	Gregrise Elfin Echo	Miss R. Walsh
1966	Holmlea Gay Harry	Stouravon Peacehill Prima Donna	Mr. J. Allen
1967	Baluch Little Shenandoah	Inverdon Endora	Mrs. Russell Roberts
1968	Baluch Little Shenandoah	Rosabunda of Costa Brava	Mr. Fullwood
1969	Wildwings Storm Petrel	Inverdon Sofia	Mrs. N. E. Staff

sensible child. A breed which is fine boned and thus needs gentle handling, but equally quite hardy.' What more could one desire?

12

Pekingese

The 'Lion' of the Toys! One of the most popular and most valuable dogs in the United Kingdom canine register. He has a fascinating history which fits in admirably with his aristocratic and dignified bearing. He is, of course, a very ancient Chinese breed and was the almost-sacred dog of the Imperial Palace of Peking, in fact only those people of royal blood were allowed to own this kind of dog and the penalty for wrongful ownership was death. However, when the Summer Palace in Peking was occupied in 1860, five of these little dogs were brought back to England. Being considered of considerable value and a great treasure, one was naturally given to Her Majesty Queen Victoria. The remaining four stayed with the Duke of Richmond, and his family raised up a strain from this nucleus. However, they did not appear in the show-ring at this time, and little was heard of them, but in the last years of the 1800's several more of these tiny 'Lion' dogs were imported into England. Crufts scheduled a class for them in 1900 but only one was entered. But after that they suddenly became popular and were the current 'rave' dogs of that era. They have never declined in popularity, always remaining one of the first three most popular toy breeds. And yet in spite of this popularity they have not been spoiled. Unlike several other very popular breeds, they have mostly retained their soundness and above all their very typical and delightful temperament. You yourself will never own a Peke, but if *he* chooses *you* as his owner, then you are lucky indeed! And once you have come to understand the unique disposition of this proud little dog then you will want no other breed—or so it is said.

Perhaps the greatest Peke breeders of all time were Miss De Pledge and her partner, the then Mrs. Lunham, who owned the Caversham Pekingese. They bred extensively and selectively, and showed regularly, and were the owners of the fabulous dog Caversham Ku-Ku of Yam who had gained no less than 39 Challenge Certificates and had been judged Best in Show at six Championship Shows. It is common knowledge that the amazing sum of £10,000 was offered for this dog to be exported abroad, and believe it or not, this offer was refused because Ku-Ku was firstly such a great pet and secondly because he was of great value as a pre-potent sire and it was felt that he could not be spared from this country. He was the son of Mrs. Lunham's Ku-Chi of Caversham who had gained nearly as many challenge certificates as Ku-Ku, had twice risen to the last four in the Best in Show ring at Crufts, and had been given the great honour of Supreme Best in Show at the West of England Ladies' Kennel Society which at that time was the greatest one-day Championship Show in the world. So certainly, present day Pekingese owe much to Miss de Pledge and Mrs. Lunham (or as she is now, Mrs. Warner-Hill, having married the well known gundog breeder and popular all round Judge in 1955).

Here is the official Standard of the breed as laid down by the Kennel Club:

PEKINGESE

GENERAL APPEARANCE—Should be a small, well-balanced, thickset dog of great dignity and quality. He should carry himself fearlessly in the ring with an alert, intelligent expression.

Head and Skull—Head massive, skull broad, wide and flat between the ears, not domed; wide between eyes. Nose very short and broad, nostrils large, open, and black; muzzle wide, well wrinkled, with firm underjaw. Profile should look quite flat with nose well up between the eyes. Deep stop.

Eyes—Large, clear, dark and lustrous. Prominent but not bolting.

Ears—Heart-shaped, set level with the skull and carried close to the head. Long profuse feathering on ears. Leather not to come below the muzzle.

Mouth—Level lips, must not show teeth or tongue.

Forequarters—Short, thick heavily-boned forelegs; bones of forelegs bowed but firm at shoulder. Absolute soundness essential.

Body—Short but with broad chest and good spring of rib, falling away lighter behind; lion-like with distinct waist, level back; well slung between the legs, not on top of them.

Hindquarters—Hind legs lighter but firm and well shaped. Close behind but not cow-hocked. Absolute soundness essential.

Feet—Large and flat, not round. The dog should stand well up on feet, not on pasterns. Front feet turned slightly out. Absolute soundness essential.

Tail—Set high, carried tightly, slightly curved over back to either side. Long feathering.

Coat—Long and straight with profuse mane extending beyond the shoulders forming a cape or frill round the neck; top coat rather coarse, with thick undercoat. Profuse feathering on ears, legs, thighs, tail and toes.

Colour—All colours and markings are permissible and equally good, except albino or liver. Parti-colours should be evenly broken.

Weight and Size—As a guide the ideal weight to be 7 to 11 lbs. for dogs, 8 to 12 lbs. for bitches. The dog should look small but be surprisingly heavy when picked up; heavy bone and a sturdy well-built body are essentials of the breed.

When choosing a puppy of this breed, there are several points to consider, apart from the general health aspect. If

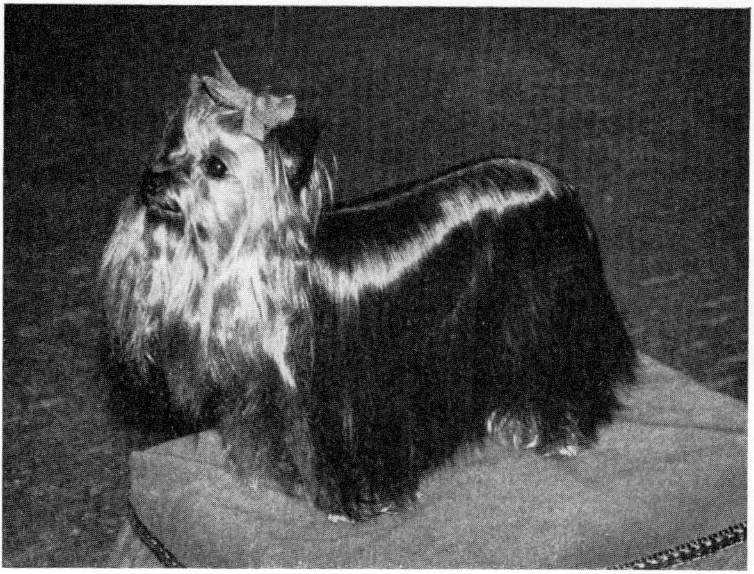

Above: YORKSHIRE TERRIER. Starr of Keeth, owned by Mrs. Copley. This is a beautiful little bitch who was made a Champion on the day this photograph was taken. Note how the coat gleams, the lovely fall of hair from the head and the straight topline. *Below:* YORKSHIRE TERRIER. A show Yorkie with his hair wrapped in tissue paper as a protection against damage to the very long falls of hair.

TOY POODLE. Rothara Lucky Laddie, owned by Mrs. Love. A bright and intelligent little dog in the Dutch Clip, with perfect black pigmentation, correct feet, good coat texture and a lovely temperament.

a dog is to be the choice then a small puppy from a small strain will be required. A dog who grows too large is not suitable for stud purposes and may not compete in the show ring. If on the other hand, a bitch is to be the choice, then a size larger is acceptable, and indeed a wiser choice for she will have just that little bit more room in which to carry her litter. The very tiny specimens are called 'Sleeve' Pekes, presumably because they could easily be taken about in the Chinese sleeve, and while sweetly pretty, they often are too small for breeding.

So to return to the choice of a puppy, a Peke should have plenty of solid bone, for while he looks small he is surprisingly heavily built when picked up. He has a shape all of his own for his head and shoulders must be quite massive with a mane which suggests the outline of a Lion. His body then should taper off to a distinct waist at the loins. His front legs must be bowed at the elbow which is contrary to many other breeds where a 'straight front' is desirable. He must possess the typical flat face with, if possible, the black mask, and his skull between the ears must also be flat with no suggestion of a dome. He has a distinctive 'wrinkle' which runs up one cheek across the nose between the eyes, and down the other cheek. Sometimes this wrinkle does not continue across the nose and is in two lines down either cheek. But it is a deep furrow and must be there. The skull is actually wider than it is deep, and of course the glamorous, large dark eyes of the Pekingese are perhaps his greatest beauty. To ensure that his glorious plume is carried well over his back, his tail should be set on high. A short back, with correspondingly short legs will ensure a good tail carriage. Because the eyes are so lustrous and large, they do give a certain amount of trouble. Great care must be taken that the eye is not injured, for ulcers form so easily. Injury can occur from a mild scratch or knock from the brush or comb, or while two Pekes are playing together. Equally, such ulcers can develop as a result of the elements, such as too much sun, too much wind, or even as the result of an upset stomach. So it behoves the Peke owner to protect his dog from possible accident or injury in this connection. An excellent lotion for daily use is Vitacoat 'Diamondeye'; otherwise, a weak solution of boracic crystals, dissolved in tepid water may be used. But it is absolutely essential that the eyes of the Peke should receive daily inspection and cleansing, which includes swabbing and cleansing of the face wrinkles.

The magnificent coat of the Peke needs very regular attention. It should be dense with a thick undercoat, and it must be straight and never curly. A good quality softish bristle brush is suitable, and the Peke should be trained right from early puppyhood to accept his daily grooming without displeasure. Most Pekes are turned on their back on the lap while the grooming of all under-parts is carried out, then sat up on the lap or on a grooming table to cope with careful and steady brushing of the back and sides, finishing with the ear fringes and the tail plume, and the profuse hair on the backs of both fore and hind legs. Pekes are seldom bathed, and their coats are kept clean and sweet by the application of talcum powder which is then carefully brushed out of the hair. Various sprays and coat conditioners are used quite extensively to develop a profuse mane and tail which are both crowning glories of this breed.

There are a large number of Breed Clubs devoted to the Pekingese. The original was the Pekingese Club which was founded in 1904. But there are also the Pekin Palace Dog Association, the London and Provincial Pekingese Club, the Pekingese Reform Association, the Birmingham Pekingese Association, the British Pekingese Club and the Invicta Pekingese Club all of which hold a Championship Show for the breed at which Challenge Certificates are awarded. In fact, there are many more Pekingese Specialist Club Championship Shows than for any other toy breed, being seven as opposed to one, or sometimes two, for the others. While many of the above Pekingese Clubs are equally important, the winners of the Dog and Bitch Challenge Certificates are noted at The Pekingese Club Championship Show held in the Spring, and the British Pekingese Club Championship Show which is usually held in the Autumn, and also the results at Crufts.

Mr. Hindley-Taylor's Puz Puz of Kyratown made a great hit at Crufts in 1968 by gaining the distinction of Best Exhibit (all breeds) bred by Exhibitor, a title any dog breeder longs to win. The Kennel of Kyratown have gained 289 Challenge Certificates with their Pekingese since the end of the war—a marvellous record. Another Peke breeder, who is right at the top, is Mrs. Bentick, for her Copplestone Pu-Zin has been judged Best in Show at sixteen Championship and Open Shows, including Bath Championship Show in 1968, and is the holder of twenty-five Challenge Certificates. He is the sire of seven overseas Champions. His father, Copplestone Pu-Zee, is the sire of seventeen champions. She has two charming sleeve Pekes called 'Bonnie' and 'Clyde' of 3½ and 3 lbs. respectively. 'Clyde' won the Puppy Stakes at Cardiff Championship Show out of an entry of 108 dogs of all breeds. Another consistent winner is Mrs. Healey's Hilleva Tudor Queen of Dropdown who held 13 Challenge Certificates, had a litter and came back to win a further certificate at Birmingham National Championship Show in 1968. Mrs. Richard Jones' Ku-Chik-Ku of Loofoo was the holder of the triple crown at Crufts 1958/59/60 and was retired at 3½ years old having 27 Challenge Certificates to his credit. Another name of great repute is that of the Alderbourne Kennel owned by the Misses Ashton-Cross. Mrs. Pilgrim's Cherlys Atom is the first parti-coloured dog to gain championship status for 14 years. Certainly the Pekingese breeders work hard in the show ring and reap rich rewards.

For many years the Pekingese was top of the Toy Breeds register by a very large majority until in 1962 the cocky little Yorkshire Terrier superseded him by a mere 250 registrations to take first place, and for two years there was very little in it but in 1966 the Peke numbers dropped by nearly 1,000.

THE PEKINGESE CLUB CHAMPIONSHIP SHOW (SPRING)

Year	*Dog Challenge Certificate*	*Bitch Challenge Certificate*	*Judge*
1964	Fu Yong of Jamestown	Margo of Kettlemere	Mrs. W-Hill
1965	Beaupres Lovely Star of Grimstoy	Cheryl of Chintoi	Mrs. McFarlane
1966	Cherangani Chips	Althaea Dodo of Kyratown	Mrs. P. B. Bull
1967	Sunshen Fan T'an	Hilleva Tudor Queen of Dropdown	Mr. S. North
1968	Goofus Buggatti	Changkim Moonbeam	Mrs. E. Pilgrim

THE BRITISH PEKINGESE CLUB CHAMPIONSHIP SHOW (AUTUMN)

1964	Ku Jin T'Sun of Laishill	Suzie Wong of Jamestown	Mr. H-Taylor
1965	Cherangani Chips	Mingshang Pekehuis Bi Jou-Shah	Mr. Stanley
1966	Mr. Redcoat of Kanghe	Oakmere Ming Kai of Brentjoy	Mr. Mitchell
1967	Cherangani Chips	Hilleva Tudor Queen of Dropdown	Mr. Bull
1968	St. Aubrey Carnival Music of Eastfield	Chrystal Crown of Changte	Mrs. E. Colomb

CRUFTS CHAMPIONSHIP SHOW (PEKINGESE)

1964	Goofus Buggatti	Margo of Kettlemere	Mrs. D. Stains
1965	Coughton Sungable of Perryacre	Cheryl of Chintoi	Mrs. W-Hill
1966	Lawrence of Wongville	Tudor Treasure of Changte	Mrs. Batchelor
1967	Mr. Redcoat of Kanghe	Belgran Jorgina	Miss P. Mayhew
1968	Puz Puz of Kyratown	Flamenco of Bonaventure	Mrs. M. Birke
1969	Cherangani Chips	St. Aubrey Fairy Ku of Craigfoss	Mrs. Wilson

However in 1967 there were still 3,774 registered Pekingese for the year in England and they now remain very steadily in 2nd place, and are placed 12th in the All Breeds register being just topped by the Golden Retriever but above the Beagle.

There are few breeds which permit of such a variety of colours for there are Red, Fawn, Cream, White, Black, Brindle, Black and Tan, and Particolour. In fact, it appears that the only two colours which are disallowed are albino and liver.

What can one say about the disposition of the Peke which would adequately and accurately sum up this fine little dog? That he is independent, jealous, autocratic, haughty and aloof, is certainly true but on the other side of the picture one finds a fearless little lion who will defend his owner with tremendous devotion, his high-handed aloofness makes one almost go on one's knee to gain his friendship, and his royal dignity of mien and bearing causes all other breeds at times to appear the veriest street urchins in comparison. And yet he can be a most charming clown, with his ears flying and his tail flowing, daring anyone to laugh *at* him instead of *with* him. And such a tremendous sport! One must own a Peke to appreciate all this. His mind works logically and intelligently, and as soon as he has worked out the answer nothing will deter him from his plans. Add all this to his breathtaking beauty and you have a dog almost beyond all others.

13

Pomeranian

The Pomeranian was, of course, a native of Pomerania in Germany, and is a descendant of the European working dogs used primarily to control sheep and cattle and also round-up reindeer. These dogs, known as Wolf Spitz dogs, were the forebears of Samoyeds, Elkhounds, Keeshonds, the little Dutch Schipperke and the Pomeranian. It does appear that some European countries specialised in various individual colours. For instance, the lovely white Pomeranian, which is seldom seen now, was a native of France, and the Red Pom is said to have come from Italy. The Pom was also known in the cold wastelands of Russia and Siberia where he was used to pull the sledges, and the Laika dog used in modern times by the U.S.S.R. for early orbiting of the earth also comes from the same forebears. These dogs were, however, much larger, weighing 40 to 50 lbs., and quite a far cry from the little Pomeranian as we know him today. It is only during the last 200 years that the Pomeranian has been carefully and selectively bred down to his present attractive diminutive size, many weighing less than 5 lbs.

It is most interesting to spend some time walking round both the British Museum and the National Gallery looking for examples of various breeds of dogs in their early stages of development. So many early breeds of dogs are found in paintings and sculpture, and of course on pieces of pottery, vases, and embroidery. There is the lovely picture *Morning Walk* by Gainsborough, dated 1785. Gainsborough seems particularly interested in this breed, for he painted his *Pomeranian and Puppy* about 10 years earlier. It is a sweet painting, the mother so alert and intelligent and the puppy obviously planning devilment. Both these paintings are in the National Gallery. There is a vase in the British Museum showing a small white pom prancing below his mistress while she is on a swing. The vase is Greek and dates back to 400 B.C. The authors were also fortunate in finding the carving of a little dog resembling a pom with a child in the Street of Tombs in Athens.

The breed really came into prominence as being the top toy breed in England when Queen Victoria took an interest in the Pomeranian. A very great lover of dogs, the Pomeranian was her first favourite, and she owned a kennel of them with the prefix 'Windsor', but they were all rather on the large size. In one of the biographies, we read that when the old Queen was dying, her little Pomeranian Turi was her constant companion and he was always on her bed.

In 1891, the original breed standard was drawn up by the Pomeranian Club and apart from size, little alteration has been made in the standard of today, over 75 years later. The Pomeranian Club was founded in this year, and Queen Victoria also became for the first time a canine exhibitor at Crufts, winning the breed class with her dog Windsor Marco.

By the early 1900's the large Poms were out of fashion, and breeders were managing to produce the really small specimens nearer to the present day type, and also some really wonderful colours had been evolved, including the beautiful sable. 'Champion Sable Mite' was the first sable to be made up to champion. The white Pomeranian is now practically extinct, and the black variety not seen too often. Both the sable and the orange appear to be by far the most popular.

After the 1914-18 War, the popularity of the lovely little Pomeranian began to wane, and his place at the top of the Toys was usurped by the Pekingese, and in 1962 the Yorkshire Terrier came up to surpass even the Peke.

Here is the official Pomeranian Standard as laid down by the Kennel Club:

POMERANIAN

GENERAL APPEARANCE—The Pomeranian in build and appearance should be a compact, short-coupled dog, well knit in frame. He should exhibit great intelligence in his expression, activity and buoyancy in his deportment.

Head and Skull—The head and nose should be foxy in outline, or wedge-shaped. The skull being slightly flat, large in proportion to the muzzle, which should finish rather fine and be free from lippiness. The hair on the head and face should be smooth and short-coated. The nose should be black in white, orange, and shaded-sable dogs; brown in chocolate-tipped sable dogs, but in other colours may be 'self-coloured', but never parti-coloured or white.

Eyes—Should be medium in size, slightly oval in shape, not full, not set too wide apart, bright and dark in colour, and showing great intelligence. In white, orange, shaded-sable and cream dogs the rims round the eyes should be black.

Ears—Should be small, not set too far apart, nor too low down, but carried perfectly erect like those of a fox.

Mouth—Teeth should be level, and should on no account be undershot, or overshot.

Neck—Should be rather short and well set in.

Forequarters—The shoulders should be clean and well laid back. The legs must be well feathered and perfectly straight, of medium length and not such as would be termed 'leggy' or 'low on leg', but in length and strength in due proportion to a well-balanced frame.

Body—The back must be short and the body compact, being well ribbed-up and the barrel well rounded. The chest must be fairly deep and not too wide, but in proportion to the size of the dog.

Hindquarters—The legs and thighs must be well

feathered down to the hocks and must be neither cow-hocked nor wide behind. They must be fine in bone and free in action.

Feet—The feet should be small and compact in shape.

Tail—The tail is one of the characteristics of the breed, and should be turned over the back and carried flat and straight, being profusely covered with long, harsh, spreading hair.

Coat—There should be two coats, an undercoat and an overcoat, the one a soft, fluffy undercoat, the other a long, perfectly straight coat, harsh in texture and covering the whole of the body, being very abundant round the neck and fore-part of the shoulders and chest, where it shall form a frill of profuse off-standing straight hair, extending over the shoulders. The hindquarters should be clad with long hair or feathering from the top of the rump to the hocks.

Colour—All whole colours are admissible, but they should be free from black or white shadings. At present the whole-coloured dogs are: white, black, brown, light or dark, blue, as pale as possible. Orange, which should be as self-coloured and bright as possible. Beaver. Cream dogs should have black noses and black rims around the eyes. Whites must be quite free from lemon or any other colour. A few white hairs, in any of the self-coloured dogs, shall not heavily penalise. Dogs (other than white) with white or tan markings, are decidedly objectionable and should be discouraged. They cannot compete as whole-coloured specimens. In parti-coloured dogs, the colours should be evenly distributed on the body in patches; a dog with white or tan feet or chest would not be a parti-coloured dog. Shaded-sables should be shaded throughout with three or more colours, the hair to be as uniformly shaded as possible, and with no patches of self-colour. In mixed classes, where whole-coloured and parti-coloured Pomeranians compete together, the preference should, if in other points they are equal, be given to the whole-coloured specimens.

Weight and Size—4 to 4½ lbs. for a dog and 4½ to 5½ lbs. for bitches.

Faults—Undershot or overshot mouths; double jointed; light eyes; off-coloured nose; a tail carried to the side; 'hare' feet.

As always with the breeds with long coats, the grooming of the Pomeranian is something which needs regular attention. The best method for this breed is a deep brushing of the coat right down to the skin once a week, with a superficial or half-groom every day. It is unwise to brush *too* vigorously *too* often, for there is an undercoat and this must not be removed, otherwise the top coat is inclined to sit flatly instead of standing out stiffly. The Pom changes coat twice a year in Spring and Autumn, and during the coat-changing period the undercoat is inclined to felt. This must be watched and all tiny mats and tags brushed or combed-out as they appear. The best type of brush is a light type with hard, stiff bristles for the once-weekly groom, and one with slightly less-hard bristles for the daily groom. A really soft brush should be used on the shorter-coated parts such as face, feet and ankles. A fairly wide-toothed steel comb, preferably one that is brass and coated with chromium, is suitable. A fine-toothed comb or a nickel one are not suitable as both tend to tear the coat. Nylon brushes are not favoured as again they pull out the coat. The coat should be groomed in an upwards direction from tail to neck, brushing the neck ruff outwards, and the breeching at the back well away from the anus.

Expert trimming needs a great deal of skill. The shaping of the ears takes time and knowledge, for the whole typical expression of the Pom can be ruined by over-trimming, and equally he can just look clumsy if not trimmed enough. There is an excellent handbook called *The Pomeranian* by Hilary Harmar which gives superb diagrams for ear trimming, and also excellent drawings dealing with the correct carriage of the tail plume which is such an important point in the Pomeranian.

Eyes must be swabbed-off daily, and ears inspected at least once a week both for any extraneous dust and dirt which may have collected and also to check that hair is not growing down into the ear.

It must always be remembered that the Pom should resemble a round ball, and therefore trimming must be carried out with this in view. The chest coat must therefore be rounded, the breechings at the back must be rounded to blend in with the round of the tail plume over the back—but this trimming must not be overdone, and should be light enough simply to suggest this roundness.

Some Poms occasionally suffer from running eyes. The cause may be obvious, such as an eyelash falling into the eye, or it may be caused by pollen, or by gusty winds. If it is hair which is causing the irritation, this may be snipped-off close to the eyelid, otherwise swabbing with Vitacoat 'Diamondeye' is quite excellent for keeping the eyes in excellent condition.

Finally, to attain a really magnificent coat on the Pom, food must be of the best quality, and if it is desired to bring a little dog into really first-class bloom he will derive tremendous benefit from grilled steak which has been brushed with olive oil. He must also have clean bedding which is frequently changed, and he must be happy. An unhappy or apprehensive dog will never have a really shining, glossy coat. It is extraordinary how many breeders groom their show dogs, taking endless trouble with sprays, conditioners, shampoos and the like, and yet they overlook the psychological side of the matter and do not realise that their little dogs are bored, bored and yet more bored! They are often shut away in their kennels or boxes with nothing to do all day so that their coats will remain unharmed. And yet if they were only given something to interest them and keep their little minds busy, then the gloss and condition would come to their coats through contentment and interest.

Pomeranians have remained 6th in the Toy Breeds Registrations for several years, being just topped by Papillons, and just above Pugs. Registration figures are singularly consistent and over eight years have varied on a slight upward trend each year from 618 registered dogs to 767.

The Pomeranian Club usually holds its annual Championship Show in May or June and the Challenge Certificate winners in each sex over the last 5 years, together with the name of the judge are given on the opposite page.

Several Pomeranians have risen to winning heights at the general Championship Shows of late. Amongst these were Mr. and Mrs. Grace's Vertona Shamrock's Joy Bells who was judged Reserve Best in Show and winner of the Toy Group at the Scottish Kennel Club Championship Show in Glasgow, and also Best Toy at Leeds Championship Show. Mrs. Dyke's Hadleigh Mighty Atom was judged Best of Toy Group at Blackpool Championship Show while Miss Harper's Cynpeg Finger of Fortune won a similar award at Paignton Championship Show. A newcomer to the breed, Mrs. Weinert, gained notice as Reserve winner of the Toy Group with her young dog Mosey The Menace of Vernlil at Peterborough Championship Show, and rapidly gaining his championship title, he is doing very well.

That great personality of the early days of dogdom, Mr. Theo Marples was the founder and first honorary Secretary of the Pomeranian Club in 1891. There are now some 85 members. Miss Hamilton of Bath, and Sir Lindsay Hogg both did a tremendous amount to foster the Pomeranian in its beginnings.

Mr. Grace of the Vertona Pomeranians gives us an outline of the true character of the Pomeranian. He says, 'This little dog is very adaptable, and being small he does not need a lot of exercise. He is very much a one-person dog and always a very lively chap. The majority of Pomeranians in this country today have very reliable temperaments, although, as in most breeds, one finds the odd one which is not very good tempered.' The authors hope this latter sentence is not taken

THE POMERANIAN CLUB CHAMPIONSHIP SHOW

Year	*Dog Challenge Certificate*	*Bitch Challenge Certificate*	*Judge*
1964	Rapture of Hadleigh	Cynpeg Aureole	Mr. Thwaites
1965	Little Model of Hadleigh	Silver Chimes of Aurum	Mrs. Anderson
1966	Honeybee of Hadleigh	Vertona Shamrock's Little Pride Girl	Miss Harper
1967	Cynpeg's Little Extra	Linchow Linthia	Mr. Flavell
1968	Haysholm Silver Toyster	Darlane's Delicious	Mrs. Weed

And here are the winners over the past years at Crufts:

CRUFTS CHAMPIONSHIP SHOW (POMERANIANS)

1964	Silver Gem of Hadleigh	Hadleigh My Cherrie of Rosebert	Mrs. Hardy
1965	Silver Gem of Hadleigh	Cynpeg Spring Fern	Mrs. Anderson
1966	Sweet Dreams of Aurum	Peachey of Hadleigh	Mrs. Barber
1967	Honeybee of Hadleigh	Cynpeg Brengarth Bella Rosa	Mr. Fullwood
1968	Linchow Lin-Tin	Vertona Shamrock Joybells	Mrs. Dyke
1969	Hadleigh Mighty Atom	Pandora of Aurum	Mrs. Robson

too literally as in their experience they have seldom found a Pom who was not sweetly dispositioned. There certainly is no more lovely picture than the sweetly pretty little Pom, in immaculate coat and bloom competing for the high honours in a ring of big brothers from all the other breeds. But apart from the show angle, who can resist their immense charm and personality, and their propensity for giving enormous affection to their owners for sometimes 16 years or more!

14
Pug

The Pug dog is an ancient breed, known in England at least since the 17th century, and almost certainly coming originally from China. The first Pugs to be seen in England were, however, a pair brought from Holland by William and Mary.

As so often in various breeds of dogs, there were two different types of Pugs, and both types had a strong following of devotees, each thinking the relevant type was that of the perfect Pug. These two strains were known as the Morrison strain and the Willoughby strain, the former was a lovely golden fawn colour, while the latter was more of a silver fawn with black mask, and a distinct black line (or trace) running down the middle of the back. These were the two original colours, but a little later Lady Brassey brought a lovely black Pug back from China with her, and this is now a very popular colour. These three colours are the only permissible ones.

The Pug enjoyed great popularity in late Victorian and Edwardian days, and in many portraits and paintings of those times, a small, rather goggle-eyed Pug is portrayed. But their popularity then drifted downwards a little in the following years until the 1940's and 1950's when the breed took an upsurge, as they were widely publicised as the chosen breed favoured by the Duke and Duchess of Windsor, and indeed there is always one or more Pugs shown at the heel of the Duke and Duchess, who certainly seem most devoted owners of this breed.

Here is the official Standard of the breed:

PUG

GENERAL APPEARANCE—A decidedly square and cobby dog. The Pug should be 'multum in parvo', but this condensation should be shown by compactness of form, well-knit proportions, and hardness of developed muscle.

Head and Skull—Head large, massive, round—not apple-headed, with no indentation of the skull. Muzzle short, blunt, square but not upfaced. Wrinkles large and deep.

Eyes—Dark in colour, very large, bold and prominent, globular in shape, soft and solicitous in expression, very lustrous, and when excited, full of fire.

Ears—Thin, small, soft, like black velvet. There are two kinds—the 'rose' and the 'button'. Preference should be given to the latter.

Forequarters—Legs very strong, straight, of moderate length, and well under the body.

Body—Short and cobby, wide in chest and well-ribbed.

Hindquarters—Legs very strong, straight, of moderate length, and well under.

Feet—Neither so long as the foot of the hare, nor so round as that of the cat; well-split-up toes; the nails black.

Tail—(Twist). Curled tightly as possible over the hip. The double curl is perfection.

Coat—Fine, smooth, soft, short and glossy, neither hard nor woolly.

Colour—Silver, apricot, fawn or black. Each should be clearly decided, to make the contrast complete between the colour, the trace and the mask. Markings: Clearly defined. The muzzle or mask, ears, moles on cheeks, thumb-mark or diamond on forehead and the trace should be as black as possible. Mask: The mask should be black, the more intense and well defined, the better. Trace: A black line extending from the occiput to the twist.

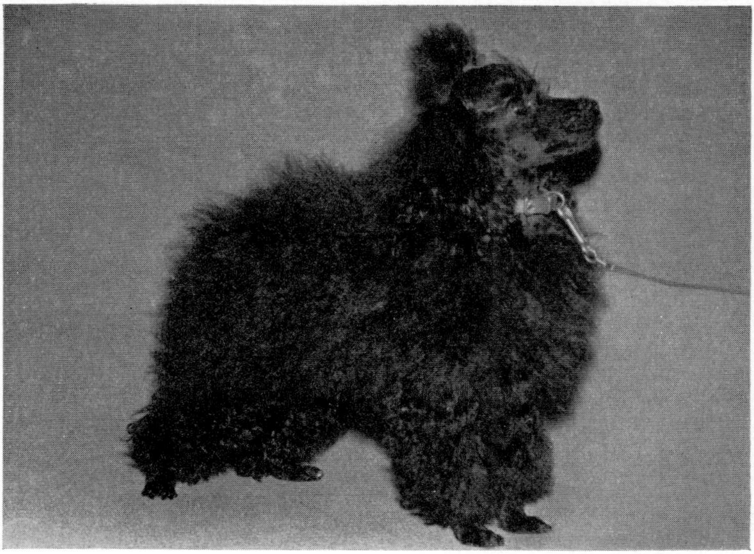

Above: TOY POODLE. Rothara Toy Flash, owned by Mrs. Sheldon, Miss Lockwood and Mrs. Brown. A short-backed, cobby puppy with a straight front and well-angulated hind quarters. *Below:* CHINESE CRESTED DOG. This is Nero of Cresthaven, owned by Mrs. Harris of the Staround Kennels. This is a rare and completely new breed. He is completely hairless except for the crest on the head, the tail plume and the feathering on the feet.

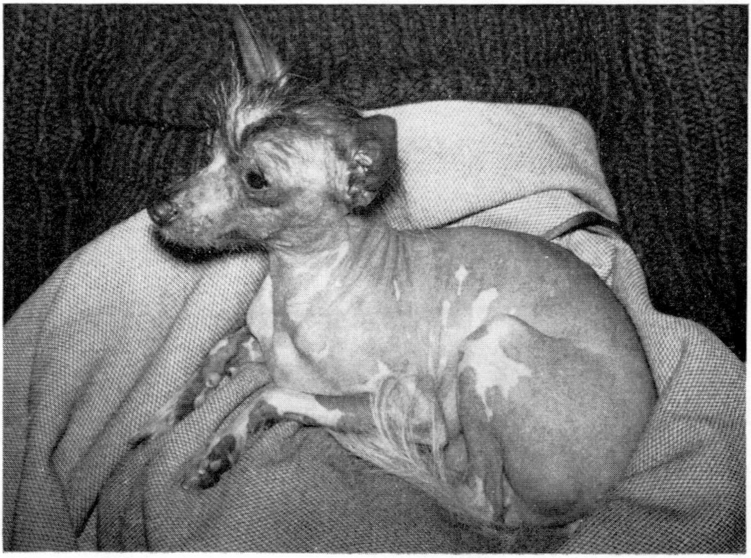

BAJAN TERRIER. Tiger, owned by Mr. and Mrs. Dusty Miller of Barbados. A sharp alert little dog now being evolved in this West Indian island. He has strong pricked ears, a moderately short coat and very expressive dark eyes.

Weight and Size—Desirable weight from 14 to 18 lbs. (dog or bitch).

Faults—Lean, leggy. Short legs and long body.

When buying a puppy of this breed, one should bear in mind that this little dog must be square and stocky, and anything in the nature of a spindly frame is not desirable. A wide chest with a really good spring of ribs should be looked for, and of course the tail should have a tight twist. The coat should be smooth, glossy, and shining with health. But really, balance in body is of paramount importance, and never must the Pug be long in back on short legs nor go to the other extreme of being high on the leg with a thin, spindly body.

Pugs are said to be somewhat difficult breeders, due to the rather massive quality of their heads, but of course this applies to other breeds such as the Pekingese, Bulldog, etc. They also have a reputation for being bad mothers, having little interest in their offspring and indeed quite oblivious to their needs in the way of hygiene. However, this should not be believed too widely because the authors know two Pug bitches intimately which have produced many families and cared for them to perfection; and also the Swedish and Scandinavian International Champion Dainty Dinah of Combwood (which was bred by Mrs. M. V. Smith) has no fewer than 19 children and 23 grandchildren in Sweden. Certainly no truth in the 'bad mother' rumour in this case! Pugs *do* snore, and there is no avoiding this fact, and to some owners or would-be owers this is distasteful, while to others it is not noticeable. Certainly the poor little Pug must not be blamed, for it is the structure of his nose, and not attributable at all to any grossness in his character, and again is not confined to this breed, for the authors owned a tiny King Charles Spaniel called 'Rex', having been born on the day of the Coronation of King George VI, and his stertorous efforts could be heard all over the house while he was sleeping (and we, as a result, were not!).

Pugs do need a little extra care in cold, damp, or foggy weather since they may be just a little prone to chestiness. Also, care must be taken over eyes as cold winds, scratches, small knocks, etc., can easily damage this rather prominent feature and start up an ulcerated condition.

Grooming the Pug calls for little expertise, and all that is really necessary is regular daily grooming with a softish fibre hound glove followed by much polishing with a velvet glove or silk handkerchief. The wrinkles on the Pug's face must have attention since they are, of necessity, large and deep. These wrinkles should be sponged-over with a baby sponge dipped in warm water and squeezed out. The wrinkles should then be dried with care, and sprinkled with a little Johnson's Baby Powder. Equally, Vitacoat 'Diamond-eye' is excellent. Bathing may be undertaken if necessary but the 'Charbon' treatment, as described in the chapter on Chihuahuas, is really excellent to keep the coat of this breed in clean and sweet condition.

Pugs for many, many years have lain fifth in the Toy Breeds popularity poll, and have not aspired to inclusion in the Top Twenty All Breeds. In 1962 over 1,600 registrations were recorded but since then numbers have dropped to the 1300's. However, some outstandingly good Pugs have held their own against all breeds in the show ring, distinguishing themselves for their soundness and delightful temperament. Of these perhaps Mrs. Spencer-Beighton's Pro Bono Pyebeta is an outstanding example, for he was Best in Show all breeds at the Ladies Kennel Association Champion Show, and also Best in Show at both the Northern Pug Dog Club Championship Show as well as the Combined Pug Dogs' Club Championship Show. Another outstanding Pug is Mr. Stanley-Young's What Oh! of Rydens which was judged Best Toy at both the Three Counties Championship Show and Cardiff Championship Show, and also Reserve Best Toy at the West of England Ladies' Kennel Society. Another good show winning type is Bo-Damnit of Ide, owned by the well-known all-round judge, Mr. Joe Braddon, which was Best Toy Dog at Birmingham Championship Show, while Mrs. Thorp's Cedarwood Blunshill Nimrod was Best Toy at Chester Championship Show. Mrs. Clifford's outstandingly lovely puppy, Hodge of Martlesham, won the Puppy Dog Class at nine Championship Shows in 1968 and was Best Puppy in Show at the Northern Pug Championship Show and of course he gained his Junior Warrant easily.

The Pug Dog Club usually hold their annual Championship Show in April, and the Challenge Certificate winners over the past five years are given overleaf.

Certainly among those exhibitors who do consistently well in the Show Ring these days must be mentioned Mr. Joe Braddon (of Ide); Mrs. Thorp (Cedarwood); Master West with his Lochranza Mr. Magoo; Mrs. Spencer-Beighton (Pyebeta); Mrs. Gifford (Martlesham); Mrs. Donaldson and Mr. and Mrs. Pickford with their Dunlossit Kennhaven Maria; Mrs. Graham's Edenderry Stacia; and Mrs. and Miss Kespar's Kennhaven Concepta of Belregis.

There are several Pug Specialist Breed Clubs, notably the Pug Dog Club, The Northern Pug Dog Club and the Combined Pug Dog Club, all of which hold an Annual Championship Show.

Certainly the Pug is a very sweet natured dog, intelligent to a degree and extremely devoted to his owners. He is also a good guard dog for he is courageous and full of fire. He has a fault it must be admitted—he is undeniably greedy! Therefore, if he is to keep his charming figure and not become too troubled with middle-aged spread, his tendency to gluttony must be curbed when his soulful and glamorous eyes stray longingly to that slice of chicken or piece of cheese, or to that succulent extra chocolate drop. However, to err is human (and probably equally canine) so one must not be too hard on the enchanting little Pug.

THE PUG DOG CLUB CHAMPIONSHIP SHOW

Year	*Dog Challenge Certificate*	*Bitch Challenge Certificate*	*Judge*
1964	Adoram Dillypin Damon	Normpug China Rose	Mrs. Coleman (D) Miss S. Weall (B)
1965	Sheafdon Ranger of Doms	Dillypin Delightful of Dobray	Mrs. Gibson (D) Maj. Gibson (B)
1966	Perkin Warbeck	Willapop Emily	Mrs. Young (D) Mrs. Thorpe (B)
1967	The Evil Weevil of Pyebeta	Empat of Winterwings	Mrs. Gifford (D) Mrs. W-Hibbert (B)
1968	What Oh! of Rydens	Cerne Hungerdale Castanet	Miss Graham

At Crufts there is always a comprehensive classification for the Pugs, and Yorkie is such a popular breed, Challenge Certificate winners over a period for the last few years:

CRUFTS CHAMPIONSHIP SHOW (PUGS)

1964	Sabu of Rydens	Jet Black of Greentubs	Mrs. Allen
1965	Edenderry the O'Donavan	Spreacombe Flying Cloud	Miss L. Weall
1966	Adoram Dillypin Damon	Hyrcania Afra	Mr. Siggers
1967	Cedarwood Blunhills Nimrod	Empat of Winterwings	Maj. Gibson
1968	Paramin Dillypin Pantaloon	Willapop Geranium	Mrs. Thorp
1969	Pro Bono Pyebeta	Phantasia of Paramin	Mrs. Cuming

15

Yorkshire Terrier

The Yorkshire Terrier is tremendously popular these days, and perhaps particularly so with our American cousins who have fallen for this fascinating Toy Breed in quite a big way.

The conclusion is naturally formed that 'Yorkies' originally came from Yorkshire but this is only partly true. This breed has been moulded by very careful and selective breeding over the last 100 years and it appears that it originated from the old Scotch Terrier which was shown as early as 1862 in the North of England. All Yorkshire Terrier breeders will have heard tell of 'Huddersfield Ben' who was born in 1865 and died only six years later. He was exhibited as a Scotch Terrier and was a magnificent ratter. He was owned by Mrs. M. A. Foster who did so much to promote the first Yorkshire Terriers.

Undoubtedly the old Clydesdale or Paisley Terrier was also used, for this terrier was a variety of soft-coated Skye Terrier, steel-blue in colour with the bright tan head, legs and feet. The present-day lovely colouring of the Yorkshire Terrier obviously emanated from this type of terrier. Many breeders are of the opinion that the tiny Maltese was also called in as a cross to get the small size.

Without a doubt the little Yorkshire Terrier must divide his allegiance between Scotland and Yorkshire, and while not being one of the oldest breeds of dogs, he can certainly look back over more than 100 years of steady, true to type breeding.

Here is the official Kennel Club Standard of the breed:

YORKSHIRE TERRIER

GENERAL APPEARANCE—Should be that of a long-coated toy terrier, the coat hanging quite straight and evenly down each side, a parting extending from the nose to the end of the tail. The animal should be very compact and neat, the carriage being very upright and conveying an 'important' air. The general outline should convey the impression of a vigorous and well-proportioned body.

Head and Skull—Head should be rather small and flat, not too prominent or round in the skull, nor too long in the muzzle, with a perfect black nose. The fall on the head to be long, of a rich golden tan, deeper in colour at the sides of the head about the ear roots, and on the muzzle where it should be very long. On no account must the tan on the head extend on to the neck, nor must there be any sooty or dark hair intermingled with any of the tan.

Eyes—Medium, dark and sparkling, having a sharp intelligent expression, and placed so as to look directly forward. They should not be prominent and the edge of the eyelids should be of a dark colour.

Ears—Small V-shaped, and carried erect or semi-erect, and not far apart, covered with short hair, colour to be of a very deep, rich tan.

Mouth—Perfectly even, with teeth as sound as possible. An animal having lost any teeth through accident not to be faulted providing the jaws are even.

Forequarters—Legs quite straight, well covered with hair of a rich golden tan a few shades lighter at the ends than at the roots, not extending higher on the forelegs than the elbow.

Body—Very compact with a good loin. Level on the top of the back.

Hindquarters—Legs quite straight, well covered with hair of a rich golden tan, a few shades lighter at the ends than at the roots, not extending higher on the hind legs than the stifle.

Feet—As round as possible; the toe-nails black.

Tail—Cut to medium length; with plenty of hair, darker blue in colour than the rest of the body, especially at the end of the tail, and carried a little higher than the level of the back.

Coat—The hair on the body moderately long and perfectly straight (not wavy), glossy like silk, and of a fine silky texture.

Colour—A dark steel blue (not silver blue), extending from the occiput (or back of skull) to the root of tail, and on no account mingled with fawn, bronze or dark hairs. The hair on the chest a rich bright tan. All tan hair should be darker at the roots than in the middle, shading to a still lighter tan at the tips.

Weight and Size—Weight up to 7 lbs.

As will have been noted, the Yorkie's coat must be parted down the middle of the back with the hair falling down over the sides of the body—the Sky Terrier also uses this style. Great stress is given to the bright tan colour and the dark steel blue—and this colouring was also a feature of the Clydesdale Terrier.

When choosing a Yorkshire Terrier puppy the usual health check must of course be carried out. These health pointers have been mentioned in other chapters and it would be a waste of space to repeat them. It must be remembered that Yorkies are born black and do not begin to change colour until around three to five months old and then the tan starts to show on the legs. The black on the back may take almost a year before beginning to turn to the lovely steel colour. Therefore it is difficult to know if your Yorkie puppy is going to turn out to be a really good colour. Suffice it to say that the puppies which take the longest time to completely clear are probably going to be the best in the end.

Balance is another important point. The back should be short and thus a cobby, sturdy litle fellow is needed, with a really straight 'top line', that is with the back bones completely straight and horizontal. A roach-backed or sway-backed Yorkie is unsightly. Size is important, for the Yorkie should be small. No breeder can guarantee the eventual *exact* height, but experience will enable him to know within a little. A good guide is to ask to see both parents if possible. The sire should be small, but the dam will in all probability be a size larger, but as long as there is not too great a size difference, the resulting puppies should keep to form. On the other hand, stamina must not be sacrificed in an effort to gain a real 'tiny', for a weakling will always be a liability. Temperament is another important point, and the puppy who is forthcoming and full of the joys of spring is worth everything, compared to the shrinking, shy little pup who jumps at every sound and at every moment, even if he may have one or two outstanding points.

To produce a Yorkshire Terrier in the right coat condition and bloom for the show ring is a work of art, and only if you relish the thought of endless grooming, shampooing, oiling, and rolling of the long hair in tissue 'curl papers', should you enter into this specialised field. If you do enjoy this type of work, then you will find it absorbing to a degree, and perserverance will undoubtedly bring success. 'Yorkie' breeders will tell you that the very best type of brush is the kind which was usually found on ladies' dressing tables and was backed either with silver or tortoiseshell. It is a softish brush with bristles three or four inches long and it just suits the Yorkshire Terrier coat. One can sometimes pick-up this type of brush from a jumble sale for 2d. or so, and if so it is really worth gold for grooming the Yorkie.

This breed should be bathed frequently and once a week is not too often. Shampoos should be carefully chosen and nothing in the nature of a hard detergent must be used. A lanolin-based shampoo is best, 'Chamoil' or 'Ko-Nutoyle' prepared by Vitacoat Ltd., of Croydon are both excellent. The coats of this breed also need frequent applications of hair tonic, and Col. Whitehead once gave the authors a splendid recipe for their show poodles, which he used with great success for his Yorkies.

Here it is:

1 oz. Tincture of Catharides
¼ pt. Bay Rum
½ oz. Oil of Rosemary
½ pt. Pure Olive Oil
1 dram. White Precipitate

These ingredients should be carefully mixed and then painted on to the hair once a week, and afterwards thoroughly brushed out. It is a slightly messy procedure but really does work wonders in growing a good coat. Otherwise Vitacoat 'Denzcote' is an excellent oil dressing enriched with lanolin, and most useful for Yorkies.

Certainly the show Yorkie does not lead the easiest of lives, for when not in the ring he must be still while his long tresses are rolled-up in pieces of tissue paper, including his long moustaches and top-knot. Quite often his little hind feet are encased in soft bootees to stop him from scratching at his 'curlers'. Of course the coat on a companion Yorkie is not encouraged by these means to grow so long, and so he leads a far more free and easy life.

The Yorkshire Terrier for a number of years now has occupied first place in the Toy Dog Registration poll, always just topping the popular Pekingese and Smooth Chihuahua. In the All Breeds chart, the Yorkie came 8th in 1962, rose to 7th and 6th in 1964 and 1965 respectively and then to 5th place, so this diminutive little ratting terrier-cum-toy is really one of the most popular dogs in Britain today. In 1968, he has moved up to 3rd place with a total of 8,842 registrations.

THE YORKSHIRE TERRIER CLUB CHAMPIONSHIP SHOW

Year	*Dog Challenge Certificate*	*Bitch Challenge Certificate*	*Judge*
1964	Elmslade Galahad of Yadnum	Phirno Magic Moment	Mde. Duchatel
1965	Buranthea's Saint Malachy	Whisperdales Phirno Carmen	Mr. Tomkins
1966	Phirno St. George	Buranthea's Luscious Lady	Miss Munday
1967	Skyrona Blue Bobby of Streamglen	Buranthea's Luscious Lady	Mr. Armstrong
1968	Murose Storm	Deebees Doncella	Mrs. Tomkins

There is also the Northern Counties Yorkshire Terrier Club, and since the Yorkie is such a popular breed, Challenge Certificate winners over a period for this Show are also given:

THE NORTHERN COUNTIES YORKSHIRE TERRIER CLUB CHAMPIONSHIP SHOW

1964	Progreso Lover Boy	Millfield Mandy	Mrs. Wilkinson
1965	My Precious Joss	Romance of Wiske	Mrs. Cross
1966	Phirno St. George	Progreso Pearl	Mrs. Stirk
1967	Macstrouds Sir Gay	Anston Lucy Locket	Mr. Groom
1968	Murose Storm	Elspeth Serenade	Mrs. Wilkinson

There is always an excellent attendance at Crufts and round the Yorkie Ring spectators are usually crushed three and four deep.

CRUFTS CHAMPIONSHIP SHOW (YORKSHIRE TERRIERS)

1964	Pagnell Peter Pan	Minerva of Jounstounburn	Mr. A. Armstrong
1965	My Precious Joss	Whisperdales Phirno Carmen	Mrs. V. Munday
1966	My Precious Joss	Templevale Jessica of Wiske	Miss P. Noakes
1967	Wedgewood's Starmist	Blairsville Tinker Bell	Mr. F. Cross
1968	Llina Star of Yadnum	Deebees Doncella	Mrs. Stirk
1969	Tolcarne Brandy Soda	Deebees Gold Penny	Miss V. Munday

The breed has its own Specialist Club, and the present secretary is Miss P. Noakes. The Club Championship Show is usually held in June and the Challenge Certificate winners over the last few years at this Show are given on the opposite page.

Of late, Mrs. Burton's Murose Storm has been doing extremely well, being judged Best in Toy Group at Manchester Championship Show, and also Best in Show at the Northern Counties Yorkshire Terrier Championship Show, while Mrs. Beech's Deebees Doncella was Reserve Best Toy at Hove, and Mr. Wood's Tolcarne Brandy Soda was Reserve Best at Chester Championship Show, as well as Best of Breed at Crufts (1969).

Mrs. Lockhart's My Precious Joss gained the distinction of Best of Breed at Crufts for two years running in 1965 and 1966.

To complete this chapter on the beautiful little Yorkshire Terrier some words of Mr. Theobald Marples from his book on Show Dogs cannot be bettered :

'Beautiful to look at, active as a kitten, vivacious as the most "Perky Pom", the perfect Yorkshire Terrier is the acme of Toy Dog virtue and perfection, looked at from every standpoint.'

16

Toy Poodle

The Toy Poodle is not strictly one of the Toy Breeds, belonging as it does to the Utility Group along with its larger brothers the Standard and Miniature Poodles. But there are many, many lovers of this tiny dog who will expect to find him featured in a book about Toy Dogs. Therefore at the risk of surprising the Toy Dog proper enthusiasts, we have included the Toy Poodles.

They are a comparatively recent variety, only being recognised by the Kennel Club since 1957. But, of course, they are purely and simply a diminutive replica of the Standard Poodle which was first registered at the Kennel Club in 1875. Toy Poodles were known in the United States of America long before they appeared in England, and the first one registered at the American Kennel Club in 1901 was Prince of Bellwood, and owned by Mr. Palmer. One of the first Toy Poodles bred in England was Lady Stanier's Seahorses Snow Queen, a tiny little white of 9″.

The French would have us believe that Poodles were of French origin and indeed until the 1940's these dogs were known as 'French Poodles', but in fact, the 'Pudle' was known in Germany and Russia as early as the mid 1500's.

Quite a number of Toy Poodles, or at any rate tiny Poodles, have made their appearance in art through the ages. There is a German portrait of about 1620 by an unknown artist showing a rather heavy German child with a small, white Poodle with a long, undocked tail. There is also a delightful picture entitled 'Toy Poodle at Dinner' and in this print a tiny white Poodle is sitting up to the dinner table opposite his mistress and being offered a leg of chicken, while the lady's maid sits to one side with only a piece of bread to satisfy her hunger! This print is dated 1818.

Cruikshank's cartoon called Monstrosities, dated 1821 shows a most extravagantly clipped little Poodle which must have been a Toy.

The Kennel Club in its fine premises in Clarges Street has a painting by Richard Ansdell of about 1860 called 'Buy a Dog, Ma'am' and this also shows a Toy Poodle. There is also an engraving of the 1800's called 'A Hot Day' and at the warm lady's feet is a Poodle which could be an oversize Toy Poodle for it looks too small to be classed as a Miniature.

A great deal of hard pioneer work was carried out prior to 1957 to evolve a tiny Poodle which would in time equal the beauty of the lovely Standard and Miniature Poodles, and indeed the breed Standard as laid own by the Kennel Club insists that the Toy Poole should be identical in every single point except size. At the present date Toy Poodles have achieved this, and there are a great many glorious little specimens who are diminutive Standard Poodles with all their elegance, soundness and pure beauty. But many of the first Toy Poodles were anything but beautiful, for they were long in back and heavy in build on short, stumpy little legs. They had round apple heads with bulging goggle-eyes. Also they did not breed true to size and continually threw back to their Miniature forebears. Mouths were also a difficulty, for often they managed to inherit rather large teeth in small mouths, therefore mouths were crowded and teeth were crooked. But the Toy Breeders battled on and in time they have evolved a lovely little dog which breeds true to type and so often takes top honours at the Championship Shows.

Unfortunately Toy Poodles have suffered tremendously from their over-popularity. In the early 1950's a few Toys were imported from the U.S.A. into England and were used very extensively as stud dogs but the type was not very good and therefore a great many faults were brought in and these were extremely difficult to eradicate. Although not proven, it has often been suggested that Maltese were at times crossed with the Toy Poodles to get dazzling whiteness.

After a few years, quite a number of Toy Poodles had been bred in England and also achieved a lot of success in the show ring, and thus it was that the improved English Toy Poodle became very much sought after by the Americans. A great many Toys were thus rapidly bred for the overseas market, and 'puppy factories' sprang up alarmingly almost overnight. Also the English pet-owners fell for the Toy Poodle in a big way. All this was extremely harmful to the breed, because the numbers of registrations soared phenomenally and a great many breeders joined in the gold rush. Selective breeding was not always considered, and many shocking specimens were sold as Toy Poodles. Soundness suffered, temperaments suffered, and the good name of Poodles suffered. A large number of breeders of other breeds also kept a few poodle bitches simply as a means of paying for the keep of their own more-difficult-to-sell dogs.

However, Toy Poodles have weathered the storm, mostly due to the perseverance and tenacity of the real lovers of the breed. Now, lovely specimens are produced and are really second to none. Far fewer shocking specimens are seen as pets, and registrations have dropped to a more reasonable figure.

Here is the official breed Standard of the Poodle and it will be seen that the Toy Poodle only differs from the Standard and Miniature Poodle in the matter of size.

THE POODLE (TOY)

GENERAL APPEARANCE—That of a very active, intelligent, and elagant looking dog, well built, and carrying himself very proudly.

Head and Skull—Head long and straight and fine, the skull not broad, with a slight peak at the back. Muzzle long (but not snipey) and strong—not full in cheek, lips black and not showing lippiness. Nose, black and sharp.

Eyes—Almond shaped, very dark, full of fire and intelligence.

Ears—The leather long and wide, low set on, hanging close to face.

Mouth—Teeth white, strong and level.

Neck—Well proportioned and strong, to admit of the head being carried high and with dignity.

Forequarters—Shoulders strong and muscular, sloping well to the back. Legs set straight from shoulder, with plenty of bone and muscle.

Body—Chest deep and moderately wide. Back short, strong, and slightly hollowed, the loins broad and muscular, the ribs well sprung and braced-up.

Hindquarters—Legs very muscular and bent, with the hocks well let down.

Feet—Rather small and of good shape, the toes well arched, pads thick and hard.

Tail—Set on rather high, well carried, never curled or carried over back.

Coat—Very profuse and of good hard texture; if corded, hanging in tight even cords; if non-corded, very thick and strong of even length, the curls close and thick without knots or cords. It is strongly recommended that the traditional Lion Clip should be adhered to.

Colour—All black, all white, all brown, all blue and all solid colours. The white Poodle should have dark eyes, black nose, lips, and toe nails. The brown Poodle should have dark amber eyes, dark liver nose, lips and toe nails. The blue Poodle should be of even colour, and have dark eyes, lips and toe nails. All the other points of white, brown and blue Poodles should be the same as the perfect black Poodle.

Weight and Size—The height at shoulder must be under 11 inches.

* * *

In the first year that Toy Poodles were recognised, that is in 1957, there were 2,169 registrations which brought them to 12th place in the top twenty poll. Then in 1958 they moved up to 7th, and in 1959 up to 3rd place. In 1960 they soared to 2nd place where they remained for four years, being surpassed only by the Miniature Poodle. In 1964 and 1965 they dropped to 3rd place, and in 1966 to 4th, but in 1967 they moved up again to 3rd place surpassing by under 100 registrations the popular Miniature. Certainly they were at their zenith in numbers, if not in quality, in 1962 with a total of 11,810 registrations. In 1968 they have dropped again to 4th place, being surpassed by the Yorkshire Terrier.

Among the pioneers of the Toy Poodle, first and foremost was Lady Stanier (Seahorses) while Mrs. Cox (Sudbrook), Mrs. Hilliard (Peaslake), Mrs. Huxham (Emmrill), Mrs. Hall (Wychwood), Mrs. Thomas (Fircot), Mrs. Proctor (Tzigane) and the authors (Rothara) all did valiant work in evolving the lovely Toy Poodle as he is today.

The grooming of the Toy Poodle calls for perserverance and a certain amount of skill. The Poodle unlike nearly all breeds, has two or three styles of hairdressing which are diametrically opposed to each other. The Toy Poodle, which is to compete in a show ring, should be styled in the traditional Lion Clip. This is not absolutely obligatory but any other clip will mean a loss of points for the length of coat, so there is really little point in trying to show a Poodle other than in the Lion Clip. In this clip the face, feet, legs and tail are clipped closely, while from the middle of the back right up to and including the top of the head a dense, heavy mane of hair should remain. The hindquarters are clipped short to approximately ½″ to 1″ in length. 'Poms' of hair are left covering ankles and wrists, with a closely-clipped band just above the ankle pom and the stifle joint, and a 'pom' is left on the tail. The real skill comes in final trimming and titivating. Poodles kept entirely as pets are seldom seen in this clip, although it is probably far more elegant and beautiful than any other style. Most companion dogs usually adopt either the Dutch Clip or the Lamb Clip.

In both these latter styles, the face and tail are clipped closely but in the Dutch Clip a narrow band is clipped from root of tail to the neck following the line of the backbone. Another band is clipped round the body from backbone, round the ribs and meeting the backbone again. The neck and throat are closely clipped. The long hair is then carefully trimmed and rounded so that it forms long 'trousers' on fore and hind legs, shoulders and hips. The hair on the head is rounded, and not gathered into a top-knot as in the Lion Clip, and a 'pom' is left on the tail.

In the Lamb Clip, face, feet and tail are clipped, but the hair on the rest of the body is trimmed evenly all over to a length of about 1″ or shorter, with just a slight fullness on the hips and shoulders. The top-knot is slightly rounded and there is a 'pom' on the tail. This is a very serviceable clip and the least difficult to maintain.

There are other clips such as the Continental clip which is a variation of the Lion Clip, the Belgium Clip, the Baby Doll Clip and others. Also the Lamb Clip is sometimes called the Curly Clip or the Astrakhan Clip.

It is absolutely essential that the Toy Poodle's coat is regularly groomed for if neglected it will quickly mat or felt. It is true that the Poodle's coat does not come out therefore he does not leave hairs over the carpets, chairs and clothes, and because of this he is completely safe as a pet for the asthmatic or one who suffers from hay-fever. But the old hair has to go somewhere and so it forms into a thick mat if neglected. Brushing should be carried out daily, with combing once a week. A 'Mason Pearson' or 'Addis' brush is ideal, while a fairly wide-toothed steel comb is correct. Poodles, if regularly groomed, do not need bathing too often, although bathing in the right shampoo will improve both the texture and the length of coat. Show dogs are bathed as often as once a week and glorious coats are the result. Messrs. Vitacoat of Croydon are specialists in Poodle shampoos and have one for every colour and condition.

A word to those dog lovers who choose a Toy Poodle—please, *please* brush every day from puppyhood onwards. It is such a sorry sight to see a neglected, matted poodle, especially as it is a breed which looks so lovely when well cared for. It only needs five minutes or even less every day, and yet if the coat is allowed to matt it will mean days of 'teazling' out the hair, and also so much pain and discomfort to the poor little Poodle.

When choosing a Toy Poodle puppy the usual check on health should be carried out. For instance, a pot belly probably means worms as does a dull or slightly cloudy eye, so look for loose skin but firm body, a bright eager eye and a cool nose. Check that the anus is clean, for a slightly sore or pink anus may mean an upset tummy through worm infestation or poor feeding. Look for a glossy coat, and avoid dull, scurfy coats which may mean the presence of parasites. Beware of the very, very tiny puppy with fragile bones, unless you are sure you can shield your puppy from almost any accident, for in this case the bones are so fragile that fractures may occur without warning. Choose a level mouth, and a puppy with an almond eye rather than a round, large one. Above all, choose a fearless, gay natured puppy who bounces at you. Avoid the puppy who hangs back and scuttles at the least sound. Some white Toy Poodles sometimes suffer from weeping eyes and the accompanying ugly brown staining—coloured Poodles have the same trouble but it isn't so noticeable. This may be hereditary and more often than not seems to skip a generation. Vitacoat 'Diamondeye' is an excellent lotion which minimises the nuisance.

The Challenge Certificate winners in each sex at the British Toy Poodle Club Championship Show over the last 5 years are given on page 116.

Among those who are never far from the top are Mrs. Barlow (Barsbrae), Mrs. Barratt (Great Westwood), Mr.

Butcher (Tuttlebees), Mrs. Conn (Montmartre), Mrs. Cox (Sudbrook), Mrs. Perry (Tiopepi), Mrs. Ringrose (Drumaids), Mrs. Strawson (Top hill), Mr. Walkden (Capilon), Mr. and Mrs. Watson (Petitbrun), Mr. Wickens (Silcresta), and Mrs. Worth (Piccoli).

Toy Poodles have had singular success when competing against all breeds, for Mrs. Perry gained Supreme Best in Show at Crufts in 1966 with Oakington Amber Sunblush, and also Reserve Best in Show at Manchester Championship Show with Tiopepi Fire Goldie quite recently. Mrs. Cox's Sudbrook Very Best of Morland was runner-up to the best in the Utility Group at Crufts in 1968, and the holder of 8 Challenge Certificates, while Mrs. Barlow's Barsbrae Branslake Harriet rose to Best in Show at Leeds Championship Show in 1967. Mrs. Barratt's Great West Westwood Montmartre Maria has won three Utility Groups, and was Best in Show at Leicester and Paignton Championship Shows and in the last four for Best in Show at Richmond Championship Show, handled by the inimitable 'Hank' Heron. Miss Wright's Aesthete Top Secret was another Best in Show winner, going to the top at Hove Championship Show, while Mr. Robb's Bhormot Bit O' Bother (now owned by Miss Bayliss) has done well by adding several group wins to his credit. The best specimens of this lovely little breed have certainly proved to all and sundry now that they can compete with any other breed for soundness and sheer quality, which is quite a feat in only twelve years of recognition.

The British Toy Poodle Club is an excellent breed club devoted to this breed, and has a membership of around 130. Mrs. Cox of Early Rivers, Prestwood, Buckinghamshire, is the efficient and hard-working secretary. The Club was founded by Lady Stanier in 1956 and a most interesting newsletter is published twice a year, and distributed free to members. There is also the London and Home Counties Toy Poodle Club, under the secretaryship of Mrs. D. Brauer (Tenaver) which flourishes and also promotes frequent shows

BRITISH TOY POODLE CLUB CHAMPIONSHIP SHOW

Year	*Dog Challenge Certificate*	*Bitch Challenge Certificate*	*Judge*
1964	Rhosbridge Golden Shred	Adastra Wonderglen Thumbelina	Mde. De Leemans
1965	Capilon Toy Toddy	Montravia Tuttlebees Winter Moonglow	Mrs. Creasy
1966	Capilon Dream Boat of Dovevalley	Oakington Puckshill Amber Sunblush	Miss Eddie
1967	Tophill Tuttlebees Timothy	Adastra Gerethkar Snow Dream	Miss Gregory (D) Mrs. Monro (B)
1968	Capilon Penthouse Pipparoo	Great Westwood Montmartre Maria	Mr. Masters (D) Mrs. Monro (B)

And here are the winners at Crufts Championship Show:

CRUFTS CHAMPIONSHIP SHOW (TOY POODLES)

1964	Great Westwood Glandore Remo	Capilon Toy Pedler	Mrs. Conn (D) Mrs. Proctor (B)
1965	Rafael of Manapouri	Viewpark Lolita	Miss Eddie (D) Ctsse. St. Croix (B)
1966	Sudbrook Sunday Excursion	Oakington Puckshill Amber Sunblush	Miss Turner (D) Mr. Cross (B)
1967	Tophill Tuttlebees Timothy	Barsbrae Branslake Harriet	Miss K. Rees (D) Mrs. Simpson (B)
1968	Montmartre Mintmaster	Sudbrook Very Best of Moonland	Mrs. Price-Jones (D) Mr. Ivan Strawson (B)
1969	Barsbrae Branslake Darty	Great Westwood Montmartre Maria	Mrs. B. Davies (D) Mrs. P. Hill (B)

for its members.

To sum up on this fascinating variety of the Poodle, this is a little dog with the elegance of a French courtier, the wickedness of a cockney street arab, the morals of a courtesan, and the bravery of a commando. It would be difficult to find a little dog with greater intelligence, in fact one must either spell words or speak a foreign language if one wishes to be secretive, and one is always somewhat surprised that the Toy Poodle does not answer back in the very best English. One day perhaps he will! And because he is so intelligent, his brain needs exercise. He *likes* to think, and he *needs* to do so. He must never be shut away to suffer the tortures of boredom and lack of companionship, either human or canine. And so this all adds up to a companion *par excellence*.

17

Two Rare Breeds—Conclusion

There is a unique breed of dog which is now coming into the limelight called the Chinese Crested Dog. There are very few in this country and they do not have a separate register at the Kennel Club, which means that when entered for a show they must appear in the Any Variety Non-Sporting class or classes, and of course so far there are no challenge certificates for them. In fact, only one appeared at Crufts in 1969. He was a four year old dog called Nero of Cresthaven, bred by Mrs. Wood, and owned and exhibited by Mrs. R. T. Harris. The Chinese Crested dog slightly resembles the Mexican Hairless dog since most of his body has no hair or only a very fine satiny sheen on the skin. But there is one significant difference, as the name implies. He has a crest of long, coarse hair on the top of the head, and long hairs on the end of the tail. This can be seen very clearly in the accompanying photograph. He has erect ears, a longish muzzle, and a sweet expression. Having so little coat he needs protection in cold, damp weather.

The second rare breed which would come within the Toy bracket is the Bajan Toy Terrier. The authors of this book spend some of the winter months each year in Barbados in the West Indies, and while there recently they had the pleasure of meeting some keen dog lovers who are engaged in evolving the Bajan dog. This dog is small, around 8 lbs. in weight, with a smooth glossy coat, prick ears, well chiselled muzzle, and a long tail with a suggestion of a plume on the end of it. He is a keen hunter after small game such as mice, lizards, crickets and frogs, is super-intelligent, and has a really delightful temperament. So far, the coat colour seems restricted to a rich honey shade. He is a good guard dog in that he tells the world in no uncertain manner when strangers are around, but immediately takes callers to his heart with true Bajan hospitality as soon as his owners arrive on the scene and are there to reassure him. Mr. and Mrs. Miller, who hail from Canada, but now live in Barbados, are concerned with various friends in evolving the Bajan Toy Terrier and so far there are several on the Island which are breeding true to type and size.

To conclude this book about the delightful Toy Breeds, one or two points suggest themselves. First of all, when contemplating ownership of one of the small Toy Breeds, do remember their size and conformation. While most Toys are very hardy, many of them do have rather fragile bones. Most of them love children, but they are not all entirely suitable for the young child nor for the rough games that will naturally take place. A bouncing terrier type is probably the better choice. Equally they are not the best choice for the energetic person who needs to take his dog for a spanking 10 mile walk every day. Many of the Toys have short legs and simply cannot cope with that type of strenuous exercise. But this is not to say that all Toys are only suitable for the role of 'old lady's lap dog'—far from it, though it must be admitted that the tiny Toy dog has much to commend itself to the elderly owner. For instance, he is light to pick up and sit on the knee, he can easily be taken on buses and under the arm into shops, he does not need a lot of exercise, and because the elderly usually have time on their hands the Toy dog quickly responds to individual attention and constant companionship. And that leads to the second essential when owning a Toy—he must have the opportunity to develop his mind. He is capable of reaching to great heights of intelligence if given the chance. Whatever happens he must not be doomed to a life of boredom. This can happen when a number of Toy dogs are kept for breeding, for there is the danger then that they will be shut away in kennels or boxes for hours on end with no companionship and nothing to do. If allowed to play with other canines their coats will suffer, their eyes may be scratched, and so it is a life sentence more or less of solitary confinement for them. A quite horrifying thought! Some breeders may not even realise what they are doing to their dogs, nor notice that the dogs' brains are stultifying and they are becoming just dull little dogs with no personality whatsoever, and yet as soon as they are allowed the companionship of both humans and canines, are allowed to enter into the family life, are talked to intelligently and given toys to interest them, they will blossom into delightful and companionable little dogs. There is no point in keeping a dog unless his personality is developed to capacity, so consider well when buying a dog whether your life and circumstances will allow you to do just that.

Do feed your Toy dog sensibly. He is small and therefore he has probably quite a small appetite, but ensure that the small amount he requires is of the best quality. Don't let him get fat because of over-indulgence in chocolate drops, sugar lumps and sweet biscuits. This only leads to discomfort for him, obnoxious breath, bad teeth and it certainly shortens his life. He will not go far wrong on two meals a day of good quality lean meat, either raw or cooked, with a sprinkling of brown bread or crumbled baked brown rusk. A drink of milky tea will not harm him. Don't forget that tinned meat contains a lot of fattening cereal, and while this food has its uses in emergency or when fresh meat has run out, it is not the food for every day.

Do groom your Toy dog regularly, particularly if he is one of the long-coated breeds. If you don't think you have the time or the inclination for grooming, then choose a short-haired, close-coated breed. A weekly check on the condition and cleanliness of eyes, ears, nails and teeth is particularly essential. This weekly check occupies only a few minutes but if neglected can cause the little dog severe and constant pain in his old age which you could so easily have avoided for him.

A dog has so much to give and asks so little in return. Do not trade on his generosity, but give him the chance to develop into the wonderful companion and comforter for which he has the capacity. If you really set about 'educating' your dog in this way you will never regret it—the only regret will be that his life is all too short.